Practical Vocal Acoustics

Pedagogic Applications for Teachers and Singers

Early voice pedagogic advice:

Play skillfully with a shout of joy.

Psalm 33:3 NASB

King David, ca. 1000 B.C.E.

Practical Vocal Acoustics

Pedagogic Applications
for Teachers and Singers

by
Kenneth W. Bozeman

VOX MUSICÆ: The Voice, Vocal Pedagogy, and Song No. 9

PENDRAGON
PRESS Hillsdale, NY

Other Titles in the VOX MUSICAE Series

No. 1. *The Art Song in Latin America* by Kathleen Wilson 1998

No. 2. *On The Interpretation of The Melodies of Claude Debussy* by Jane Bathori 1998

No. 3. *Interpreting The Songs of Jacques Leguerney: A Guide For Study and Performance* by Mary Dibbern, Carol Kimball, and Patrick Choukroun 2001

No. 4. *Carmen: A Performance Guide* by Mary Dibbern 2001

No. 5. *The Tales of Hoffmann: A Performance Guide* by Mary Dibbern 2001

No. 6. *Faust/Romeo et Juliette: Two Performance Guides* by Mary Dibbern 2006

No. 7. *Manon: A Performance Guide* by Mary Dibbern 2011

No. 8. *Werther: A Performance Guide* by Mary Dibbern 2012

Library of Congress Cataloging-in-Publication Data

Bozeman, Kenneth.
  Practical vocal acoustics: pedagogic applications for teachers and singers
/ by Kenneth W. Bozeman.
      pages cm. — (The voice, vocal pedagogy, and song ; No. 9)
  Includes bibliographical references and index.
  ISBN 978-1-57647-240-8 (alk. paper)
  1. Singing—Acoustics. 2. Voice—Acoustics. 3. Singing—Instruction and study—
Technological innovations. I. Title.
  MT820.B795 2103
  783'.043071—dc23
                          2013015839

Contents

Foreword

The study of human sound has a long history, harking back, I suspect, to ancient documents on oratory by Cicero, Seneca, Quintilian, and others. The history of the singing act itself is more compressed, but with remarkable achievements over a relatively short period of time. To garner some understanding of how far we've come in the investigation of the human vocal instrument, one may try to imagine the enormous excitement surrounding the invention of the laryngoscope, along with the first glimpse of the vocal folds in action, and compare that with the rather commonplace status of stroboscopy today. Manuel Garcia's invention began an initially timorous, self-conscious courtship of science and pedagogy that ultimately merged into a marriage where stormy beginnings have, I think it's safe to say, matured into a healthy, symbiotic relationship. The offspring of that union is a proliferation of research and writing about the human voice that has virtually exploded in the last half of the twentieth century and into the twenty-first. We have now attained a point of historical perspective at which we can trace a scientific/pedagogic ancestry that generates a clearer understanding of the present and offers direction for the future.

The book you are holding in your hands is an important contribution to the literature, a unique and at the same time necessary expansion of the study of voice. A cursory reading of the title, may lead one to think of acoustics in an external sense, that is, space acoustics and their effect, and perhaps studio voice recording. The subtitle, however, narrows the definition toward an internal orientation, requiring examination of voice as an acoustic instrument consisting of power source, sound source, and sound modifiers. It differs from typical voice pedagogy texts in that it does not offer discrete chapters on breathing, registration, articulation (*per se*), interpretation, and the like; rather, it focuses on the pedagogic implications of the voice as an acoustic phenomenon. If much of the material seems more directly oriented toward the male singing voice, it is because men experience more complex acoustic phenomena than do women. Nonetheless, a great deal of female acoustic strategy is offered as well. Additionally, acoustic technology such as *VoceVista* and the *Madde* Synthesizer is being increasingly used as instructional aids in the voice studio, and Bozeman, who, if not a pioneer, is certainly an authoritative champion in the application of the latter, offers the reader expert tutorials in each.

For a few decades now, I have known Kenneth Bozeman both personally and professionally as a highly respected singer, scholar, teacher, and author. I have been present at several of his workshops and master classes, and it has been my privilege to have published some of his work in the *Journal of Singing*. That research, along with a great deal of additional material, has found elaboration and expanded context in this book, and I can think of few more highly qualified to offer a study of this nature. In a subject area where one soon can sink in a sea of unfamiliar terminology, technology, and concepts, Bozeman navigates with a lucid, common sense approach. There is much information, cogently arranged and clearly presented in accessible language, at the same time avoiding pitfalls of oversimplification. His chapter on formants, for example, is one of the most easily understood treatments of the subject of which I'm aware, a paradigmatic primer that should be required reading for all singers and singing teachers.

To continue the genealogic metaphor introduced above, Bozeman's commitment to distill matters from voice science—especially acoustics—into practical voice pedagogy, illustrates a lineage to the late iconic Richard Miller, whose insistence that all voice science regarding the *act* must ultimately serve the *art* of singing forms the philosophic and pedagogic underpinnings of this volume. This is a very good book, written by an expert teacher for teachers.

Richard Dale Sjoerdsma, PhD
Editor in Chief, *Journal of Singing*
Professor Emeritus, Carthage College
Kenosha, Wisconsin
April, 2013

Preface

At the 1981 convention of the National Association of Teachers of Singing in Minneapolis, Minnesota, Thomas Cleveland presented a paper on the relationship of the singer's formant frequency to voice category. During his presentation a synthesized tenor voice was played singing an F major scale on the vowel /ɑ/. Remarkably, the tenor's vocal quality migrated through the color changes associated with male *passaggio*, though no changes in the vocal tract formants or source input had been programmed other than the change of pitch (fundamental frequency). Though *passaggio* was not the focus of the presentation, at that moment I was struck with the notion that the timbral shifts of vocal cover were not due to changes in laryngeal register, rather to some resonance phenomenon not yet understood. Thus began my journey into the area of vocal acoustics.

Eight years later in a voice lesson with the late Richard Miller during a sabbatical at Oberlin, my voice "turned over" while singing an /e/ vowel on D4. I had previously thought that the male voice began to prepare for the upper voice during the *zona di passaggio*—roughly D4-G4 for a tenor—but only turned over near the *secondo passaggio*, at G4. I was also surprised at the quality of the vowel, which sounded odd to my internal hearing. I asked Richard if what I had just done was acceptable. He had me sing the passage again, and without further explanation said that it was fine. That was the second major step in this journey. I was practicing during the sabbatical in the new laboratory Richard was developing at Oberlin at the time, and was regularly using the Kay Elemetrics *Sona-Graph* 5500 with its real time spectrography. In very short order I realized that the voice turned over and "closed" in a parallel relationship to the first formant locations of vowels. It would be a few years before I knew precisely what the factors were, but from that point on my teaching of male *passaggio* was changed.

Over the next decade I tried a few times to interest members of the voice science community in testing this hypothesis, but without success. I didn't know that at about the same time Donald Miller and Harm Schutte were observing this and other acoustic phenomena in their lab in Groningen, Netherlands. It was not until I was provided with Svante Granqvist's *Madde* voice synthesizer that I could prove with precision what I had long suspected: that the male voice turns over when the second harmonic rises above the first formant. By this time Miller and Schutte had documented this and related phenomena, and in a subsequent visit to Lawrence University where I teach, Donald confirmed my observations. I have since enjoyed very informative conversations with Donald and a number of other voice scientists, most of whom now acknowledge the phenomenon of the F1/H2 turn of the voice.

I am not a voice scientist. I am a voice teacher. It is not my intention with this bit of personal history to encourage voice teachers to presume to know what we don't—there's enough of that already in every profession—rather to realize that we each bring something of great value to the conversation. While voice teachers need to be open to learning from the voice science community, and willing to relinquish ideas that run counter to reality, we also have vitally important things to contribute. Ongoing open and honest collaborations between voice teachers and voice scientists—both of whom are thoughtful and humble enough to consider perspectives other than their own—are needed to advance the pedagogy and art of singing.

This present text is an attempt to distill insights and principles emerging from voice research that have proven fruitful for studio pedagogy, and to present them in a manner that is accessible to the general voice community. It aspires to contribute both to better pedagogy and to more productive, better informed, mutually respectful and beneficial conversation between the pedagogic and scientific communities.

I am indebted to many souls for what I have learned in the area of voice acoustics, from the writings of William Vennard, Johan

Sundberg, Ingo Titze, and Donald Miller (who also spent a week as a guest in my home discussing aspects of the book and advancing my understanding, especially of female resonance strategies), to enlightening conversations with scientists Ron Scherer and David Howard, and with knowledgeable voice colleagues such as Richard Miller, Scott McCoy, John Nix, Christian Herbst, Stephen Austin, and Dan Ihasz. I thank several who read drafts of the text and gave very helpful feedback: Christian Herbst, Donald Miller, John Koopman, Richard Sjoerdsma, Stephen Austin, Scott McCoy, Steven Spears, and Dale Duesing.

I also owe a special thanks to my good friend and the voice editor at Pendragon Press, Kathleen Wilson, for urging me to write this text in the first place, for her subsequent enthusiasm for the project, and for insisting that I make it clear and accessible to those less familiar with the jargon of voice science.

I thank my students from whom and through whom I have learned over the years, especially those who contributed the recorded exercises for the enclosed DVD*: Luke Randall, Davey Harrison, Willson Oppedahl, Phillip Jindra, Jon Stombres, Mitchell Kasprzyk, Cayla Rosche, Paige Koebele, Natasha Foley, Jenna Kuchar, and Emily Flack. I also thank my colleague David Berk, our expert in instructional technology, who gave generously of his time and expertise in producing the DVD.*

*(now available at http://www.kenbozeman.com)

Finally I am grateful to my son Christopher for help with graphics and illustrations, and to my wife, companion, best friend, and fellow voice teacher, Joanne, for countless pedagogic conversations, editing help, common sense counsel, and moral support.

Kenneth W. Bozeman
Frank C. Shattuck Professor of Music
Lawrence University Conservatory of Music
Appleton, Wisconsin
May, 2013

About the Author

Kenneth Bozeman, tenor, Frank C. Shattuck Professor of Music at Lawrence University Conservatory of Music in Appleton, Wisconsin, (1977-present) holds performance degrees from Baylor University and the University of Arizona. He subsequently studied at the State Conservatory of Music in Munich, Germany on a fellowship from Rotary International. He is chair of the voice department at Lawrence, where he teaches voice and voice science and pedagogy.

Mr. Bozeman has received both of Lawrence University's Teaching Awards and was awarded the *Van Lawrence Fellowship* by the Voice Foundation and NATS in 1994 for his interest in voice science and pedagogy. He is currently the chair of the editorial board of the NATS *Journal of Singing*. He is frequent presenter on voice acoustics—especially as applied to male *passaggio* training—for venues including the Voice Foundation, the Physiology and Acoustics of Singing Conference, the Pan European Voice Conference, and the European Voice Teachers Association. Mr. Bozeman presented on acoustics for NATS at the 2012 and 2014 conventions and for the 2015 Winter Workshop, and was a master teacher for the 2013 NATS Intern Program at Vanderbilt University. Mr. Bozeman was an active recitalist and performer of oratorio, having performed with the Milwaukee Symphony, the Wisconsin Chamber Orchestra, the Green Lake Music Festival, the Louisville Bach Society, and on Wisconsin Public Radio. His students have sung at major opera houses, including Deutsche Oper Berlin, New York City Opera, Santa Fe, Houston Grand, San Francisco Opera, and the Metropolitan Opera.

Chapter 1
Introduction

Voice teachers have been addressing vocal acoustics in some manner for as long as there has been voice instruction. Given the history of excellence in singing, singers, and teachers, the historic empirical approach clearly has had success. However, our scientific knowledge about and understanding of vocal acoustics has grown exponentially in the last sixty to eighty years, and will certainly continue to be refined by the growing number of ongoing collaborations between voice scientists and voice teachers interested in voice science. With sophisticated yet inexpensive sound analysis technology now widely available, more voice teachers are curious about its potential value for the studio, and are seeing the need to understand and be well informed about the acoustics of vocal registration—at the very least, as a means to more efficient pedagogy, but also as an essential element of voice pedagogy courses. There are several excellent texts available that delve deeply into the physics of vocal acoustics *(See Selected References)*, and on instructional technology and pedagogic application, but there is still a need for texts that explain the pedagogic implications of acoustics in a manner accessible to the majority of teachers and students. This book represents an attempt to place principles emerging from voice science in a clear and practical pedagogic context for voice teachers and voice pedagogy students. An effort has been made to distill from the science of vocal acoustics those factors that are essential for teachers at the beginning of the twenty-first century to understand and that are most likely to be productive for improving our pedagogic efficiency, and to present them in language that is generally accessible. It is the author's view that while refinement of our scientific understanding of vocal acoustics will surely continue, the basic elements presented here will be immediately helpful and are sufficiently well-established to survive further developments. This text will be limited to acoustic information that is relevant to teaching and will not address in any detail non-acoustic aspects of singing. It is also based primarily in the aesthetics and practices of the Western classical singing tradition, though many of the acoustic principles presented are relevant for and applicable to other vocal styles.

Tools

First a brief word about technology in the studio: There is a growing array of software applications available for studio use. For those who object to the amount of voice science and instructional technology invading the studio, consider these observations: the teacher that can't teach a good voice lesson without it won't be able to teach a good voice lesson with it. Most technology is merely sophisticated feedback that can give more concrete evidence of that for which good teachers were already listening or looking. This is no different in principle than the use of a mirror, an audio recording device, or a video recording device. The teacher is still just as dependent on a refined ability to hear and observe what the student is doing, but instructional technology can improve the specificity of instruction, the learning curve of students, quickly settle arguments over sounds just made, and generally make teaching more efficient. Of course one can certainly imagine use of the same technology becoming intrusive, too prominent, or inefficient if not well managed, much like an obsession with the mirror might be.

Later chapters will explain two excellent instruments of instructional technology: the *Madde* voice synthesizer, and the *VoceVista* sound analysis program. A number of points in the text will be illustrated by suggested explorations using the *Madde* voice synthesizer (see Appendix 1, p. 117). Possible studio uses of *VoceVista* will be explained and illustrated in a subsequent chapter. In order to understand and effectively use these instructional tools, the teacher and student will need a basic understanding of vocal acoustics. Readers sufficiently informed about harmonics and formants are encouraged to read the instructional technology chapters first and then do each *Madde* exploration as it is suggested in the text. (Seeing and hearing the *Madde* explorations in some cases dramatically and convincingly illustrates the principle being discussed.) Others may find it more productive to return to the *Madde* explorations only after first processing the chapters on harmonics and formants.

Chapter 2
Harmonics Primer

Musical Tone

Musical tones are sounds usually made of many frequencies, all of which are multiples of a lowest common denominator frequency, called the **fundamental frequency.**[1] Each of these frequency components is called a **harmonic.** Together they form a sound pressure pattern (**pressure waveform**) that repeats itself at the frequency of that lowest common denominator. Our perception of that fundamental frequency is called its **pitch.** The relative strength of all frequency components—the fundamental and the higher frequencies or harmonics—determines the "color" or "quality" of the tone. Harmonics are numbered from the lowest as H1, H2, H3, etc. Since musically notated pitch is logarithmic in relation to frequency, the intervals between successive harmonics of the harmonic series decrease in size starting with an octave, a perfect fifth, a perfect fourth, a major third, a minor third, etc., as shown in figure 1.

Figure 1: Intervallic relationship of the first eight frequencies of the harmonic series of the pitch C3.

Voice Acoustics

Voice acoustics are comprised primarily of two factors: a **voice source** or vibrator, which produces a set of harmonics, and a **vocal tract filter** or resonator, which selectively strengthens or weakens frequencies that are introduced into it by the voice source. The effect

---

[1] Throughout this text, explanations of the terms printed in **bold typeface** can be found in the Definitions section starting on page 104.

of the interactions between these two factors is the primary concern of acoustic voice pedagogy. This chapter (Harmonics Primer) will explore the former—the voice source and its contribution, which constitutes the acoustic raw material from which the voice is made. A later chapter (Formants Primer) will explore the characteristics of the vocal tract as a resonator, followed by a third chapter (Formant/Harmonic Interactions) that examines how these two factors coordinate and interact.

Voice Source Harmonics
In non-noisy styles of singing,[2] voice source sounds are made up of sets of approximately harmonic frequencies produced by the vibrator (the vocal folds), whose frequencies are determined by the pitch being sung (in other words, usually by the composer). In the typically vibrant tone of Western classical singing, these frequencies oscillate regularly above and below the target frequency set (the intended pitch) at a rate of approximately six times per second, creating the phenomenon of vocal vibrato. There may also be some noise element, but the better or "cleaner" the phonation, the higher the harmonic to noise ratio—that is, the less noise there will be. In an excellent tone, there is no perceivable noise, in other words, no non-harmonic frequency components. Before being resonated by the vocal tract, harmonics from the voice source "**roll off**" or weaken in power the higher they are above the first harmonic or fundamental frequency at a rate that is affected by several variables, but ideally at about 12 decibels (dBs) per octave. (See figure 2.) This un-resonated, pitched "laryngeal buzz" is vital yet surprisingly unattractive (see *Madde* exploration 1).

***Madde* Exploration 1: the un-resonated voice source (See Appendix 1, p. 117)**

Voice Source Harmonic Characteristics
The number and strength of audible harmonics from the voice source are determined by four factors: mode of phonation, laryngeal register, intensity, and fundamental frequency.

---

[2] The tonal ideal of Western classical singing pursues perceptually "pure" tones—at least in its vowels. Noise involves the presence of non-harmonic frequencies in a sound. Some vocal styles include noise elements as a part of the sound palette.

4

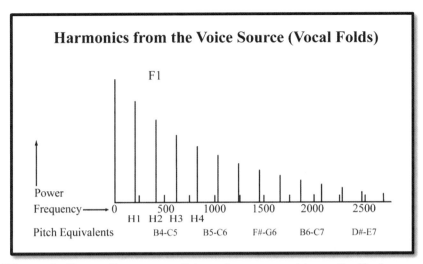

Figure 2: Power Spectrum of the voice source with a roll off of ca. 12 dB's/octave. A power spectrum displays power on the vertical and frequency on the horizontal.

Mode of Phonation

The **mode of phonation** has to do with the relationship of three factors: breath pressure, airflow, and glottal (valve) resistance. Of these, the amount of breath pressure (via torso compression) and the degree and type of glottal adduction are the active, causal, controlling factors, with the amount of airflow being the result. These factors can be modeled in a **phonation equation:**[3] breath pressure/airflow = glottal resistance. While there are many possible ratios between these factors, they can either be in balance, or imbalanced in one of two ways: too much airflow or too much glottal resistance.

- **pressed phonation** (a phonation with excess glottal resistance) has a moderate fundamental frequency (F_o) or first harmonic (H1), a gradual roll off in power, and thus relatively

---

[3] The numbers used in the phonation equation are not actual measurements of pressure, flow, and resistance, rather they are symbolic of values, with the number 1 modeling an ideal amount of each for any given situation. Of course actual values will vary necessarily by circumstance (a dramatic tenor loud C5 versus a countertenor mezzo forte C5, for example), but an ideal balance as well as various imbalances can be conceived and modeled for each circumstance. Such modeling is useful for considering the nature of an imbalance and for devising corrective strategies.

more and stronger high harmonics. It is therefore metallic or overly bright in timbre. Ex.: $1/.5 = 2$

- **breathy phonation** (a phonation with excess airflow) has a moderate to strong F_o(H1), but a steep roll off in power, and therefore fewer and weaker high partials, and often some air noise element. It is therefore airy, fluty, and sometimes noisy in timbre. Ex.: $1/2 = .5$

- **flow phonation** has a strong F_o(H1), a moderate roll off (about twelve decibels per octave) and a good set of high harmonics. It is therefore balanced in timbre. Ex.: $1/1 = 1$

Laryngeal Register

Laryngeal register refers to the muscular adjustment of the vocal folds for pitch regulation. This is primarily controlled by the **thyroarytenoids** (TA; vocal fold shortening, thickening muscles that make up the body of the vocal folds) and the **cricothyroids** (CT; vocal fold stretching, thinning muscles that lie partly outside of the larynx). Shorter, thicker, looser folds vibrate at lower frequencies and are "chestier" in laryngeal register, while longer, tauter, thinner folds vibrate at higher frequencies and are "headier" in laryngeal register. (See Laryngeal Registration Revisited, p. 93, for more detail and for training suggestions.)

- **chestier** (shorter, thicker) laryngeal adjustments have a **vertical phase difference** (a greater depth of vocal fold contact with an abrupt, undulatory contact from lower to upper vocal fold edge in each cycle) creating a more complex **pressure waveform** with more, stronger high harmonics. It is therefore inherently brassier in timbre. This thicker vocal fold shape is increasingly referred to as **vibrational mode one**.[4]

- **headier** (longer, thinner) laryngeal adjustments "chop" the airstream more simply (little to no vertical phase difference) and less abruptly, creating a more sinusoidal pressure wave

---

[4] *Vibrational* mode refers to a characteristic of vocal fold shape and vibratory pattern that is not only the result of the degree of muscle participation by the various laryngeal muscles that shape the vocal folds, but is also affected by aerodynamic and acoustic factors that can trigger a "toggling" from one vibrational mode to another.

pattern with a strong F_o(H1), but fewer, weaker high harmonics. It is therefore flutier in timbre. This thinner vocal fold shape is referred to as **vibrational mode two**.

Intensity[5]

- **louder** phonations have more harmonics, and stronger high harmonics.
- **softer** phonations have fewer harmonics, with a steeper roll-off and weaker high harmonics.

Fundamental Frequency (H1) (roughly the equivalent of the pitch)[6]

- a lower F_o (lower pitch) has both more, and more "closely spaced" harmonics within audibility. For example, a man singing C3, an octave below middle C, will have 32 harmonics within the range of the keyboard.
- A higher F_o (higher pitch) has fewer, more "widely spaced" harmonics. A soprano singing a "high C" (C6) will only have four harmonics within the range of the keyboard.
- The number of harmonics within timbrally significant audible range (roughly within the keyboard or below ca. 4200 Hz) has major implications for vocal resonance, resonance management strategy, as well as for intelligibility.

Madde **Exploration 2: the effect of mode of phonation and range on source harmonics**

Take-Away Message for Harmonics

Voice source harmonics comprise the essential raw material out of which the resonated sound is made. The resonator (vocal tract) does

---

[5] Intensity is the physical property for which loudness is the percept. While the terms are not synonymous (as with frequency and pitch: see footnote 6 below), for most practical pedagogic purposes, we needn't be concerned with the distinction.

[6] Frequency and pitch are not synonymous terms, since pitch is our perception of a sound pressure pattern often comprised of multiple frequencies, and can be "flatted" or "sharped" from the actual fundamental frequency by resonance factors. However, for most practical purposes, singing teachers needn't worry about this distinction.

not make any sound; it only reinforces, or not, sounds introduced into it. Therefore the singer needs a good set of harmonics, freely gotten, appropriate in balance and roll off for the pitch, dynamic, and affect he or she is given to perform. This healthy set of harmonics is dependent upon the establishment of flow phonation through clean, complete, firm but gentle glottal closure, an effective, responsive breath/voice connection, and appropriate laryngeal registration for the situation.

Breath management and even laryngeal registration are topics that will not be covered to any great extent in this text. Nonetheless, effective coordination of breath with phonation, as well as an ability to make the laryngeal adjustments in vocal fold shape necessary for all pitches of the range, are requisite, foundational factors in establishing optimal resonance. That said, we will learn that idealized resonator adjustments can significantly assist both breath management and vocal fold vibration.

Chapter 3
Overview of the Changing Theories
of Vocal Resonance

Our understanding of how the vocal tract resonates the harmonics from the voice source (vocal folds) has evolved considerably over the last fifty years. Before an explanation of the details of current theory is given, a cursory overview of how theories of vocal resonance have developed will provide some context.

Resonance

Resonance is the tendency of an object or system (like the air contained by the vocal tract) to respond (oscillate) more strongly to particular frequencies introduced into it. The oscillation of frequencies—such as the harmonics from the voice source—that are at or near the resonance peaks of the vocal tract will be greater than those frequencies that are farther away from those resonance peaks.

Coupled Helmholtz Resonators

Early models of vocal resonance were based on a theory of two successive, coupled **Helmholtz resonators**: the pharynx and the oral cavity, with a narrowing created by a tongue bulge dividing them. The basic principle in determining the "pitch" (resonance frequency) of each resonator was thought to be the size of the contained air space and the relative size of the exit of that space. The larger the space and the smaller the exit, the lower the frequency of its resonance would be. Therefore an /i/ with its large pharyngeal space and narrow, rather frontal exit to the mouth created a low "pitched" first resonance. That resonance would then be coupled into a small space in front of the tongue hump with a larger exit (relative to the small oral space) at the lips, creating a higher "pitched" second resonance. The explanatory effectiveness of this theory was best for front vowels like /i/, but less convincing for back vowels like /u/, which has a low first resonance even though it has a relatively small pharyngeal space. The coupled resonator theory left the tuning mechanism of higher resonances somewhat in question. It also did not account for the **epilaryngeal tube**, nor consider the functioning of the entire vocal tract as a single tube with multiple resonances. Nonetheless, the observation that larger spaces with smaller opening exits contribute to lower resonances is still useful, as is the sense that the pharynx is more associated with the first resonance and the oral cavity with the second.

Linear Source-Filter Model

A more recent model—the **linear source-filter model**—presents vocal acoustics as being comprised of three elements: a power source (breath pressure and flow), a source vibration (formed at the vocal folds), and a resonator (the vocal tract), which filters the input from the source, selectively strengthening or weakening harmonics from the vocal folds. This model recognized that the tuning of vocal tract resonances could be more effectively explained from a single, **quarter-wave resonator** model. A quarter-wave resonator is a tube closed at one end (the glottis) and open at the other (the lips). Such a resonator naturally resonates a sound wave four times its length, hence its name, "1/4-wave" resonator. Uniformly shaped quarter-wave resonators also reinforce sound waves that are odd numbered multiples of this lowest resonance frequency. This model was assumed to be strictly linear: a power source (breath) bringing the vocal folds into vibration, generating a set of harmonic frequencies which then proceed up and out. Some of these source harmonics are then selectively strengthened by the resonances of the vocal tract before finally being radiated from the lips. Though the vocal tract is not a uniform tube, this model is largely accurate and explanatory, but falls short of explaining the potential non-linear interactivity of resonator and vibrator.

Non-Linear Source-Filter Model

The most recent model proposes a **non-linear source-filter model** with the potential for interactivity or non-linearity. In certain circumstances (more on this later: See Non-linear Source-Filter Theory Revisited, p. 43) acoustic energy passing through the filter can be productively reflected back onto the source, assisting the efficiency and power of the voice source/vibrator.

Chapter 4
Formants Primer

Vocal Tract

The vocal tract is a tube that is open at one end and mostly closed at the other. As mentioned above, that makes it a quarter-wave resonator, with a primary resonance or standing wave at the frequency of a sound wave that is four times as long as the vocal tract. And again, such resonators also have resonances at higher frequencies, whose standing wavelengths within the vocal tract are odd numbered multiples of 1/4: 3/4, 5/4, 7/4, etc. Hard-walled resonators—like brass instruments—will only resonate rather specific, narrow, harmonic frequencies. Being a soft-walled tube, the vocal tract has resonances with wider frequency **bandwidths** than other quarter-wave instruments. This enables the vocal tract to reinforce source harmonics that are even in the vicinity of its peak resonance frequencies. Source harmonics that lie mid-way between widely spaced vocal tract resonances will however be significantly weakened, if not lost altogether.

Formants

Since the vocal tract is a shapeable, non-uniform tube, its natural resonances are tunable—within limits—to wavelengths other than those listed above. These resonances are called **formants**[7] in most voice science literature. Formants then are the natural resonances of the vocal tract. There are typically only three to five formants low enough in frequency and strong enough in intensity to be of great aural significance. Their frequency locations are the result of the length and shape of the vocal tract/tube (Titze, 1994). Tube *length* determines the general location of the entire formant set:

---

[7] In some voice acoustic disciplines, the term formant is not used for the peak resonance frequencies of the resonator, rather for the spectral peaks of the radiated sound, reflecting how the resonator has filtered voice source harmonics. For such disciplines, tube resonances (the potential of the tube to filter and transfer sound from the glottis to the lips) and formants (the actual spectral peaks of the radiated sound) would only be identical if the resonance peaks are tuned precisely to source harmonics, or conversely, if harmonics land precisely at resonance peaks. However, most singing voice literature does not make this distinction, using the term formant as equivalent to vocal tract resonance.

- the longer the tube, the lower the frequencies of the formant set, and the more that fall within aural significance.
- the shorter the tube, the higher the frequencies of the formant set, and the fewer that are aurally significant.

Since where the formants lie depends primarily upon tube length and determines overall vocal timbre, then tube length is a significant factor in determining and maintaining the vocal category or **Fach** (the voice type) of the singer. Singers who allow their larynx location—and thereby, their tube length—constantly to change with pitch change will achieve neither a unified timbre nor a consistent timbral category (sopranos in their extreme high range excepted).

Number of Formants

Formants are theoretically infinite in number, but only three to five (depending upon voice type or vocal tract length) are of much timbral significance, falling within the heart of audible range, roughly, the pitch range of the keyboard (below ca. 4200 Hz).[8] Within that range, basses typically have five formants, sopranos three, and most everyone else four. Formants are numbered F1, F2, F3, F4, etc.

Madde Exploration 3: formant resonation of source harmonics; harmonic/formant crossings

The Roles Formants Play

Vowel Formants

The first two formants (F1, F2) are the most responsive to changes in vocal tract shape, and are therefore tunable to differentiate and define vowels. They are therefore referred to as the **vowel formants**. They are tuned primarily by adjusting where the vocal tract is internally

---

[8] Human audible range can extend to ca. 20,000Hz, which is over two octaves beyond the range of the keyboard (to ca. Eb10). While frequencies that lie beyond the piano keyboard are present in certain consonants, and can contribute to tonal timbre in some singing styles, they do not usually play a significant role in Western classical voice pedagogy, the focus of this study.

narrowed by a bulge or hump of the tongue, and by the size of the tube exit (lip shape). An internal narrowing nearer to the front (nearer the lips) causes a lower first formant and a higher second formant. A narrowing nearer the back causes a higher first formant and a lower second formant. Lip rounding lowers both formants, especially the first, and lip spreading raises both formants, especially the first. This tuning of the shape of the vocal tract is generally referenced in speech literature as **articulation.**

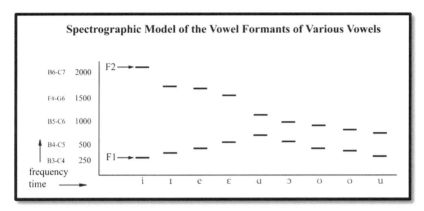

Figure 3: Spectrographic model of the first two vocal tract formants, the vowel formants.

Vowel Modification
Moving the first two formants around amounts to adjusting or even changing the vowel by reshaping the vocal tract, ideally while preserving its length. This is usually what is meant by the term **vowel modification.** Since this involves intentional reshaping of the vocal tract from habituated speech postures, this might more accurately be called *active* **vowel modification.** (More later.)

The Roles of the First Formant
The first formant determines depth or fullness of timbre, and the openness-closeness dimension of vowels. Furthermore, as we will learn, all *acoustic* (as distinct from laryngeal) registration events are caused by or related to interactions between the first formant and voice source harmonics.

13

Depth or Fullness of Timbre

The **first formant,** being the lowest resonance of a voice, is most responsible for **depth** and **fullness** of timbre, i.e., the strength of lower harmonics in the sound (also described as warmth or round-ness). First formants (F1s) lie in the two octaves between C4 and C6, usually in contact with the treble clef (D4-G5). The first formants of any given voice typically vary by about an octave across all vowels, from the lowest F1 of an /i/ vowel to highest F1 of an /ɑ/. It is necessary to have at least one source harmonic near the first formant frequency peak in order to be fully resonant and to have timbral depth. This becomes especially important for the upper range of treble voices. If no source harmonic is being resonated by the first formant, the tone will lack fullness and be thin or shrill. The possible exception to this is the whistle register, which is typically much less full in timbre anyway, though in some singers remarkably resonant. In the latter case, the fundamental or first harmonic is probably being resonated by a cluster-ing of formants one and two or possibly by the second formant. It is useful to know that the lower the frequency of F1 relative to the vowel being sung, the more open the throat is.

Openness-Closeness Dimension of Vowels

The frequency of the first formant also determines the **openness** or **closeness** of a vowel. **Close vowels** such as /i/ or /u/ have low first formants. **Open vowels** such as /ɛ/, /ɔ/, or /ɑ/ have high first formants. Therefore the higher the formant the more open the vowel, the lower the formant the closer the vowel. As with colors, where a range of frequencies is identified by a single color designation (red, for example), so it also is with vowels. Within a single vowel identity, the higher the first formant tuning, the more open the pronunciation will sound, and the lower the first formant, the closer the pronunciation. As the first formant moves up or down, at some point vowel identity will shift to that of a neighboring vowel, just as shades of red at some point morph into a shade of orange or of purple. For example, if raising F1, /i/ eventually shifts to /ɪ/, /e/ shifts to /ɛ/, etc., or vice versa if lowering F1.

Harmonic Interactions with the First Formant

Whenever a source harmonic passes through the first formant there is an audible effect (some degree of closing or opening of the timbre with an accompanying, simultaneous **passive vowel modification**), which is perceivable as an **acoustic registration** phenomenon. These harmonic-formant crossings and their acoustic effects are often avoided by moving the first formant, an instinctive response that must be trained away for classical singing timbre (more later). All acoustic registration events have primarily to do with harmonic interactions with the first formant.[9] It is therefore pedagogically very useful to know the first formant locations of the cardinal vowels and the general frequency location contour of the entire first formant set (see figure 9, p. 26 and Appendix 2: Approximate F1 Locations by Voice, p. 124).

The Roles of the Second Formant

The second formant plays a role in clarity of vowel definition, the front-back dimension of vowels, in upper voice resonance strategies of men, as well as in middle voice resonance strategies of women.

Vowel Clarity/Definition

Although both first and second formants participate in defining a vowel, the **second formant** is perceptually more responsible for **clarity** of definition. This is perhaps due to its perceptual association with the oral cavity, or to the fact that the second formant varies more consistently across all vowels than the first formant, whose location is duplicated across the front and back vowels. For this reason, it is an instinctive though poor resonance strategy to exaggerate oral shape differences to improve clarity of diction. Excessive orality is usually at odds with *chiaroscuro* **balanced resonance** (page 18 below). The perceptual dominance of the second formant in vowel identity is also apparent in onomatopoeic sound associations: words descriptive of high sounds (such as tweet, scream, sizzle), often contain vowels with

---

[9] Acoustic registration refers to audible timbral shifts associated with some perceived change in registration, which are not due to laryngeal mechanism, but rather are due to changing relationships between source harmonics and vocal tract formants. Harmonic interactions with the second formant—which are often also crucial to acoustic registration events—are dependent upon and in that sense secondary to harmonic interactions with the first formant, though no less important.

15

high frequency second formants, while words descriptive of mid (pound, shout) and low (moan, groan) sounds contain vowels with mid and low frequency second formants.

Front-Back Dimension of Vowels

The second formant is also responsible for the perceived **front** or **back dimension** of a vowel. Front vowels, such as /i/, have a high second formant while back vowels, such as /u/, have a low second formant. Second formants lie approximately between A5 and D7, that is, roughly two to three octaves above middle C, varying about an octave across all vowels within a given voice. The front/back perception is due to the proximity of the second formant to either the first formant (as in /u/) or third formant (as in /i/). Proximate formants are mutually reinforcing. Like party animals, when they get together, they make more noise! Therefore a low second formant would reinforce the first formant, boosting the low frequency components of the timbre and creating a "back" vowel. A high second formant would reinforce the **singer's formant cluster**, boosting the treble components of the timbre, creating a "front" vowel. Front-back dimension corresponds also to tongue shape: a fronted tongue creates a smaller frontal space and a higher second formant, while a less fronted tongue creates a narrowing nearer the back of the oral cavity, a larger frontal space, and a lower second formant. We will see later that the front-back dimension of vowels does not necessarily correspond directly to their perceived "placement" locations (sensation of vibrational locus).

Second Formant Strategy for Male Upper Voice

The second formant also plays a prominent role in the upper voice resonance strategy for a significant percentage of premier male singers, especially tenors. When the second harmonic of the voice source loses power as it surpasses the frequency peak of the first formant, professional male singers will often modify resonance in order to boost the second formant by tuning it to an available, higher source harmonic in order to achieve an especially ringing top (Donald Miller, 2008). (More on this later: see Second Formant Strategies, p. 29.)

16

Singer's Formant Cluster (SFC)

Higher formants (formant three and higher) cluster under certain conditions (a low larynx, an open throat, and a narrowed **epilaryngeal** exit). This forms the so-called **singer's formant cluster (SFC)**, that ringing quality associated with professional classical singers that gives them carrying power over orchestras, etc. (Sundberg, 1974; Titze & Story, 1997). It is most characteristic of male voices, but also of females in their middle and lower registers, that is, for sung pitches below ca. D5. The singer's formant cluster lies within the top octave of the piano (C7 and C8), usually in the middle of that octave (2400-3200 Hz.) where the human ear is most sensitive to loudness. This is because the human ear canal is also a quarter-wave resonator whose primary resonance is in the 3000-4000 Hz range. Any harmonics entering the ear canal within those frequencies will receive a strong resonance boost on the way to the eardrum. Once a sung pitch itself is high enough to project, vocal resonance becomes less dependent upon the singer's formant cluster and increasingly dependent upon the strength of the fundamental frequency being resonated by the first formant. For this reason, the singer's formant cluster plays a decreasing role in the upper registers of treble voices.

Relationship of the SFC to Vocal *Fach*

The location of the singer's formant cluster is primarily determined by the length of the vocal tract, and is significant for timbre and thus for vocal *Fach* (voice category) determination. In general, the longer the tube, the lower the SFC, and the lower the resultant vocal *Fach*; the shorter the tube, the higher the SFC and *Fach*. Keeping tube length stable across range and vowels is therefore a key factor in unifying and stabilizing the timbre and perceived *Fach* of the voice.

Relationship of the SFC to Resonance Balance and Interactivity

Balanced resonance involves some degree of parity between the strength of high and low partials of the radiated sound, at least for pitches below ca. D5. This is usually accomplished by a balance between the depth-responsible first formant and the ring-responsible singer's formant cluster. The creation of the singer's formant cluster requires a six to one differential between the area of the pharynx and the outlet of the epilarynx (Sundberg, 1974; Titze & Story, 1997). This condition is only met when the larynx is comfortably low, the laryngo-pharynx relaxed open, and the **aryepiglottic sphincter** narrowed. Those very conditions create a **convergent resonator**, a relatively lower F1, and ensure timbral depth. This means that the singer's formant cluster is depth-dependent. That is to say, the SFC is not just about achieving "ring," but actually only occurs when accompanied by timbral depth, creating the balanced resonance of *chiaroscuro*. While a voice may have strong higher formants and be "bright" in timbre, it does not have a true singer's formant cluster unless the higher formants are drawn together by an accompanying depth. In this way SFC creates a situation of acoustic **reactance** and **inertance**, interactivity factors that can result in more overall acoustic power for less breath pressure or glottal resistance.

Effect of the Piriform Sinuses
The **piriform sinuses**, which branch off to the sides of the **epilarynx**, have the effect of negating resonance in the 4-6000Hz region, thereby highlighting the singer's formant cluster and suppressing any formants that lie just above it (Delvaux & Howard, 2014).

Vocal Tract Sound Transfer Characteristics
As shown earlier in figure 2, p. 5, a power spectrum displays power on the vertical and frequency on the horizontal. A **spectral envelope** out-lining the resonance characteristics of a particular vocal tract shape would then display that vocal tract's ability to transfer acoustic energy (sound) from the glottis to the outside world. (See figures 4 and 5.)

Formants Relative to the Keyboard
If the frequency dimension of a power spectrum is adjusted to be logarithmic, like pitch on a piano keyboard, the relative locations of formants are more easily grasped by musicians. Figure 5 below shows the same vowel as figure 4 above it (an /i/), adjusted to a logarithmic scale. The high location of the second formant puts all formants other than the first near or in the top octave of the piano, leaving a large "valley" between the first and second formants of the /i/. This explains its relative "brightness" but also its potential thinness if no harmonic is being resonated by its first formant. With the lowest first

formant and the highest second formant of all vowels, a well produced /i/ can have excellent *chiaroscuro* timbral balance.

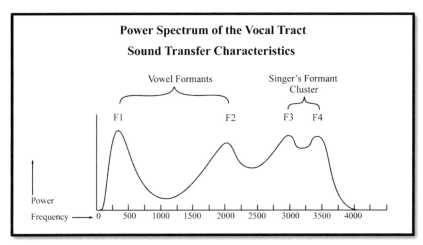

Figure 4: A power spectrum of the vocal tract for the vowel /i/ with a linear frequency scale.

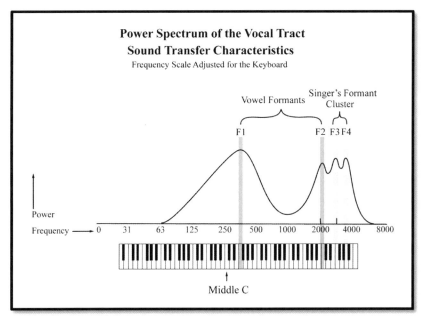

Figure 5: A power spectrum of the vocal tract for the vowel /i/ with a logarithmic frequency scale adjusted to the keyboard.

19

Chapter 5
Harmonic/Formant Interactions

Vocal resonance is the result of the interactions between voice source (vibrator) harmonics and vocal tract formants (tube resonances). In general, we want approximate matches between our formant tunings and those harmonics of the pitch being sung that are available for resonation. Harmonics may lose power more rapidly on the high side of a formant frequency peak due to reactance (Titze). Since we have no control over the location of the harmonics (they are determined by the pitch we are required to sing), the main factor that we can affect in order to be resonant is the location (tuning) of the first two formants. The Western classical singer will want the location of the higher formants to be as stable as possible for consistency of overall timbre and *Fach*. However, the first two formants can be tuned to resonate available harmonics.

Harmonic/First Formant Interactions
While interaction between source harmonics and all formants is impor-tant, interactions with the first formant are especially important. If no harmonics land within the first formant bandwidth, ideally below the formant frequency peak, the overall sound will be weaker and thinner. There needs to be at least one harmonic near F1 to be resonated by it in order to have fullness and depth. If there are two or more harmon-ics below the first formant, i.e., when singing lower pitches, there is little need for **formant tuning**, since in that situation there will usually be plenty of harmonics available for resonation by the first, second, and higher formants. With higher fundamental frequencies, harmonics are more widely spaced, leaving fewer harmonics within range of the first two formants to be resonated. Therefore more attention to formant tuning becomes necessary when singing higher pitches.

Possible Formant/Harmonic Interactions
There are four possible interactions between formants and harmonics: 1) a formant can allow a moving harmonic to pass through it (opening or closing the timbre); 2) a formant can move across a stable harmonic

(a vowel change on the same pitch); 3) a formant can track a harmonic (yelling, belting, or whooping); and 4) a formant can be "detuned" away from a harmonic (F2 upper treble voice strategy).

Timbral Opening and Closing

Whenever a source harmonic passes through and above the first formant, there is an aural effect described as a **closing** of the timbre. Whenever a harmonic drops below F1 the timbre can be heard to **open** to some degree.

Open Timbre

When two or more harmonics lie at or below the first formant, the timbre is described as **open timbre** (*voce aperta* in Italian), the more harmonics below the first formant, the more open the timbre. In other words, open timbre occurs when singing an octave or more below the first formant of the vowel being sung. Open timbre might be described as bright, straightforward, clear, fresh, exposed, coming more directly out of the mouth, and—if low enough in pitch—buzzy. If taken too high, open timbre becomes blatant or spread as in a yell.

When the first formant is tuned to the second harmonic, or conversely, as the second harmonic approaches the peak frequency of the first formant, an **F1/H2 acoustic coupling** occurs, which forms an especially strong form of open timbre, characterized by ringing clarity and power. This is such a strong acoustic coupling, that we instinctively adjust for it when power and projection are needed.

Yell Coupling

If this F1/H2 open timbre coupling is maintained or tracked above the normal F1 location of the vowel being sung by raising the first formant in tandem with the rising second harmonic, the singer has moved into **yell timbre.** This is a valuable resonance strategy when needed in life, and is quite common in musical theater, popular, folk, and world music idioms, but yell timbre is avoided in Western classical singing. These non-classical vocal styles can be said to exploit the power and "naturalness" of more or less skillful yelling. The ability to yell is apparently an inherited, universal, and strong survival instinct. Overcoming this instinct is crucial in training young males to negotiate their *passaggi* successfully with Western classical timbre. On the contrary, carefully managing a form of it is crucial to training musical theater belt timbre.

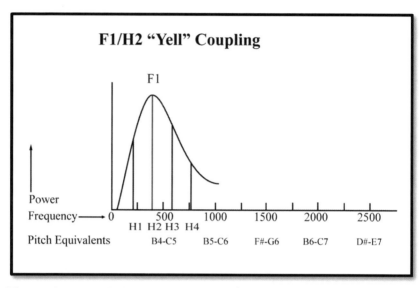

Figure 6: Open timbre coupling of F1/H2: If this coupling is carried higher by tube shortening, it creates the "spread" timbre of a yell.

Yell Characteristics

Yell timbre and function is accomplished by raising the first formant through tube shortening (larynx raising), pharynx narrowing, and mouth widening, i.e., by creating a **divergent** resonator shape. The first two of these maneuvers are accomplished by activating swallowing muscles which raise and constrict the laryngopharynx, narrowing the throat, preventing the use of singer's formant *chiaroscuro* timbre and influencing the vibrator function toward pressed phonation. Furthermore, yelling is typically done on open vowels

22

like /ɑ/ or /ɛ/, because their high F1 locations and inherently more divergent shape make them more compatible with the acoustic requirements of the yell (try yelling on a pure /u/!). The yell is chest register (TA) or **mode one** dominant. These maneuvers result in the raised and forward reaching chin of the young male accommodating his rising larynx, plus a widened vowel posture.

Close timbre
When the second harmonic crosses above the first formant, the timbre is heard to close or **turn over**. This crossing is the primary *acoustic* registration event of male voices. Close timbre (*voce chiusa*[10] in Italian) is variously described as seeming domed, tipped, smoother, higher in sensation in the head, and somewhat less direct (covered). This occurs when the sung pitch is less than an octave below the first formant of the vowel being sung. It is a necessary component of Western classical upper voice training, since unlike other vocal styles, it enables the upper range to occur without loss of timbral depth or warmth.

Turning over is accomplished by retaining depth (tube length), vowel shape, and relative vowel closeness—all of which maintain the F1 frequency location—until the second harmonic has surpassed the F1 frequency. It is accompanied by some degree of **passive vowel modification**, a change in the vowel quality that is the result of maintaining the tube shape while the pitch and its harmonics move, in contrast to *active* modification, which involves a deliberate shape change with a resultant retuning of formants.

Whoop Coupling
When H1 (the pitch one is singing) reaches the frequency of the first formant, there is a **strong F1/H1 coupling**. This is called whooping or hooting, and is characterized by a "hootier" full, deep timbre, which is dominated by the fundamental frequency, resonant, yet smoother

---

[10] The term *voce chiusa* is used by some to denote the generally convergent resonance strategy that results in *chiaroscuro* timbre and singer's formant cluster, and *voce aperta* to denote a generally divergent resonance strategy.

and less brassy than open timbre. It may seem more centralized in the head, being dominated by the first harmonic and first formant.

Whoop Characteristics

Whooping is accomplished by tuning the first formant to the $H1(F_o)$, that is, to the pitch being sung. It is falsetto (CT) or **mode two** dominant, tends toward flow phonation, facilitates laryngopharyngeal space and a convergent (open to the back, narrower to the front) resonator shape. It is primarily done on close vowels, especially /u/, because their low F1 frequency locations facilitate F1/H1 coupling (it is difficult for most males to whoop on open vowels unless very high). Since women eventually sing pitches at or above the first formants of all of their vowels, they are often operating in whoop mode, especially in Western classical singing.

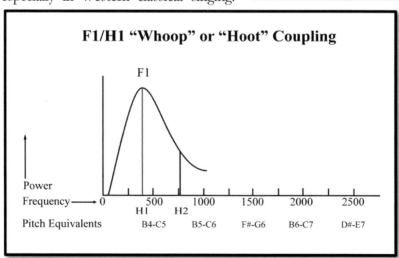

Figure 7: The F1/H1 coupling of whoop timbre, very characteristic of female classical singing.

24

Yell and Whoop Frequency

These two resonance strategies are inherently strong acoustically and therefore occur universally among humans. For example, when desiring to make a lot of sound at sporting events or enthusiastic celebrations, humans either yell or whoop. If done to excess, either can cause hyper-functional wear. However, whooping is the lower pressure, lower risk, vocally healthier of the two options. Cultural acceptability is another matter. "Bravo!" in whoop mode is not likely to catch on.

Turning Over

The most prominent and pedagogically relevant of these various harmonic/formant interactions for men is the crossing of the second harmonic (H2) above the first formant (F1). This is the **primary** *acoustic* **register transition** of male voices, and, at least for the open vowels, has been termed vocal cover or turning over. It is associated with the laryngeal shift from what has historically been called chest to head voice (or chest to middle/mixed registration or a lighter version of laryngeal mode one). As mentioned before, this transition also generates a timbral shift that could be described as **passive vowel modification**, since it causes a subtle closure and rounding of the

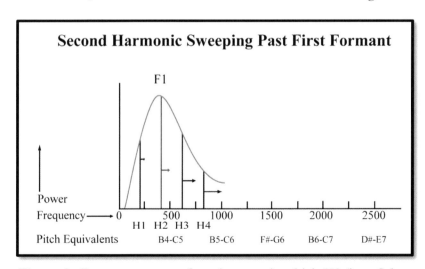

Figure 8: Power spectrum of turning over in which H2 (in red) has just surpassed F1.

vowel timbre. This modification is accomplished not through a shape change, but through changing relationships between moving source harmonics and stable vocal tract formants.

The Pitch of Turning

The **pitch of turning** is determined by the location of the first formant of the vowel being sung, which is affected by how openly or closely the vowel is being pronounced. The pitch of turning is slightly less than an octave below the first formant of the vowel, since H1 is an octave below H2. That is, when you are singing a given pitch, its second harmonic is an octave higher. Notes below the pitch of turning for a given vowel (an octave or more below the first formant of that vowel) will be in open timbre. Notes above the pitch of turning for that vowel (less than an octave below the first formant of that vowel) will be in close timbre. If turning over were the result of laryngeal registration events rather than first formant locations, one would expect a voice to turn over at the same pitch for all vowels. It does not. Maintaining that view is no longer a viable pedagogic position.

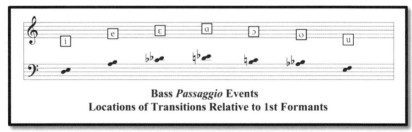

Bass *Passaggio* Events
Locations of Transitions Relative to 1st Formants

Figure 9: Approximate first formant locations of the cardinal vowels (modeled on the staff in a musician user-friendly way) for a bass voice. Each vowel formant (containing its IPA symbol) is placed in a box on the treble clef, with the pitches at which the voice would turn over or close notated on the bass clef below each vowel. Note again the overall contour of the set of vowel formants. This can be adjusted up or down for other voice categories. From highest to lowest voice category, formant locations only vary by about a 4th or 5th with average soprano formants spanning approximately G4-G5 and bass formants approximately C4-C5 (see Appendix 2, p. 124).

As mentioned above, open vowels (like /ɑ/) have high first formants. Close vowels (like /i/ or /u/) have low first formants. The more

26

openly you pronounce a vowel, the higher its first formant will be, and the higher it will turn over. The more closely you pronounce a vowel, the lower its first formant will be, and the lower it will turn over. The ability to hear the turning of the voice, knowledge and anticipation of the locations of turning, and the willingness and ability to allow that timbral shift to occur, all are extremely helpful in training male *passaggio* and female lower voice.

Madde Exploration 4: open and close timbre

From Turning to Whoop

There is an octave between H1 and H2. Therefore, if tube length and shape are kept constant—in other words, if the frequency location of F1 is kept constant—there will be just under an octave between turning over, where H2 rises above F1, and arrival at full whoop timbre, where H1 matches F1. An acoustic challenge is posed by the octave separation between H1 and H2: immediately above the turn, where H2 begins to drop in power as it relinquishes the advantage of F1 resonation, H1 is still too far below F1 to match the power H2 just lost. This loss in power can be exacerbated—especially in women—by an earlier shift in laryngeal registration toward vibrational mode two, with its greater CT (head voice) dominance, weaker glottal resistance, and steeper roll off in intensity of upper partials.

Resonance Strategies between Turning and Whoop

There are three basic first formant strategies used in this transitional range:

> 1) active vowel modification that lowers F1 to precipitate whoop sooner;
>
> 2) maintaining tube shape and F1 tuning; and
>
> 3) active vowel modification that raises F1 to postpone or avoid whoop.

Overlapping with these F1 strategies in this transitional register from turning to whoop are second formant strategies: it is precisely here that F2 couplings with a higher harmonic are often sought to maintain or boost intensity. Some women alternatively cluster F1 and F2 enough—by means of a back open vowel—to continue boosting the second harmonic lying between them.

Lowering F1 through Active Vowel Modification

If a closer vowel, a closer pronunciation of the same vowel, or some other throat opening, timbral deepening strategy (such as tube lengthening) is used that maximizes resonator convergence for the vowel being sung, F1 will be lowered. This will cause a more rapid ascent into full whoop timbre (an F1/H1 match). In other words, it will reduce the interval between turning and whooping to rather less than an octave. This is a common strategy of treble voices (women and countertenors) in Western classical singing, where the opulent head voice of whoop timbre is desirable throughout most of the range.

Maintaining Vocal Tract Shape

Maintaining vocal tract length and vowel closeness (and thus F1 frequency location) when ascending above a vowel's point of turning will result in a gradually closer, headier timbre until full whoop timbre is achieved about an octave higher. As the fundamental frequency (H1) ascends the slope of the first formant and begins to dominate the timbre, tonal sensations may seem increasingly centralized, since whooping is generally felt in the head and vertical pharyngeal column. However in the lower range of this acoustic register, overall intensity may need assistance from the second formant resonating a higher harmonic or from a clustering of the first and second formants, resonating the second harmonic that lies between them. If appropriate for the voice type and musical style, intensity may also be helped by retaining a more robust (mode one, "chestier") laryngeal registration above the turn.

Raising F1 through Vowel Opening

Alternatively, once the voice has turned over into close timbre, the vowel shape can be gradually opened, starting a step or two above the point of turning while staying in close timbre. This strategy will postpone arrival in full whoop timbre and retain a turned over, yet more robust timbral mix. It involves raising the first formant by opening the vowel shape in a manner that keeps F1 positioned well above H1—the pitch being sung—(avoiding full whoop timbre) but still below H2 (avoiding yell timbre). This approach effectively lengthens the pitch interval between turning over and whoop timbre to more than an octave, in some cases avoiding arrival into whoop coupling altogether. As the vowel is opened to raise F1, it will be important that tube length—and timbral depth—not be compromised by larynx raising.

As mentioned above, in Western classical singing, trained women prefer the first two strategies, leaving vowels close or even closing them more in order to sound headier and fuller—to reach full whoop timbre—lower in the range. Men tend to prefer the third strategy, opening the vowel somewhat above its point of turning (especially on close vowels) in order not to proceed into falsetto/whoop timbre. Many premier male singers also seek out F2/harmonic couplings to boost the virile ring of the voice for more exciting, professional operatic top notes.

Second Formant Strategies

As just mentioned, it is in the range between turning over and arriving at whoop timbre—for open vowels, approximately the pitch range of the treble clef—that strategies involving a more prominent second formant are employed by many professional singers, especially males. This is most likely due to the large intervallic distance between H1 and H2, as compared to the relatively smaller distances between higher harmonics and their "trailing" harmonics. For example, when H3 surpasses F1, H2 is less than a perfect 5th behind and already sufficiently within the bandwidth of F1 to be resonated by it. However, when H2 crosses through F1, H1 is almost an octave below. The resultant loss of power can be countered if a higher harmonic is within the bandwidth of F2. As Donald Miller has pointed out, for front vowels which have a high F2 frequency center, this is likely to be H4 or higher. With the back vowels, which have a low F2, this is likely to be H3. This seems to be a feature of many premier tenors, generating an especially ringing top range. Others maintain a stronger singer's formant cluster to achieve ring. Similar strategies in female singers can be appropriate for the lower middle voice, but for the upper middle voice can cause an overly brilliant sound and a reluctance to relinquish the

F2/H3 (or F2/higher harmonic) dominance in order to establish the F1/H1 dominance of full whoop timbre. F1/H1 dominance is essential to opulent operatic head voice for pitches nearing the top of the treble clef and above. In any case, in order to have the fullness and depth necessary for timbral balance, once H2 has surpassed F1, F1 will need to resonate H1 to some sufficient extent.

First Formant Tracking of H1 (F1/H1)

Normally a skillful singer would not want to sing a pitch (F_o, H1) higher than the tuning of the first formant (F1), since the tone would lack depth and fullness. Therefore, when a pitch is sung above the normal location of a vowel's first formant, the vowel should be actively modified to raise F1 in tandem with the rising pitch in order to maintain full whoop timbre.

There are two ways to raise the first formant: tube shortening and vowel opening. Vowel opening is the better option. Opening a vowel involves increasing its overall shape divergence, while trying to preserve something of its characteristic shape relative to other vowels. For example, if it is a tongue-fronted vowel (tongue humped near the front teeth rather than flat), some tongue fronting and frontal narrowing will be preserved, even as the vowel is opened. The higher the pitch being sung, the more subtle any vowel distinctions become, but some thought/intention of the intended vowel can assist intelligibility remarkably high in the singing range. If it is a lip-rounded vowel within speaking range, some hint of lip rounding remains above speaking range—as compared to a non-lip rounded vowel—until quite high.

Tube shortening raises *all* formants and therefore changes timbral *Fach*. It should generally be avoided except for the extreme high range of females (ca. B5 and above). By that pitch, the ability to raise the first formant by vowel opening alone has been exhausted, so that elevating the larynx is the only remaining means of raising F1. At that point, laryngeal elevation does not necessarily compromise vocal freedom, since tuning F1 to H1 provides beneficial interactive feedback to the vibrator, reducing the amount of glottal resistance necessary.

Besides, the vocal *Fach* of singers attempting such stratospheric frequencies is rarely in question.

Such vowel opening F1/H1 formant tuning is used by males (other than countertenors) only for the vowels whose first formants lie within their singing range, such as /i/, /u/, and /y/. As mentioned above, trained males tend to avoid whoop timbre altogether by keeping the first formant above the pitch they are singing through vowel opening, unless they are seeking a pure head tone or falsetto timbre for occasional special effect. But untrained or less skillful males often neglect to open sufficiently when singing above the first formant locations (ca. E4 to G4) of their close vowels (/i u y/) resulting in timbral thinness and more effortful phonation.

Untrained males also often raise the larynx on close vowels such as /i/and /u/ even after those vowels have closed, i.e., within the octave below the vowel's first formant. In this case they are attempting to stay in a more robust laryngeal adjustment without opening the articulation of the vowel when singing pitches that approach its first formant. Maintaining a low larynx and close pronunciation in that situation would normally result in the timbre becoming increasingly "heady." Raising the larynx to avoid that whoop timbre causes a shallower timbre and pressed or constricted phonation. Opening the vowel shape *within* close timbre by opening the mouth while maintaining a relaxed and settled larynx will facilitate robust timbre and postpone or avoid whoop timbre. Treble male voices (countertenors) will need to use the same formant tuning resonance strategies as female voices.

31

Chapter 6
Female/Treble Voice Resonance Strategies

Women and treble males (countertenors), whose ranges lie primarily in the treble clef, face both different laryngeal registration issues and formant/harmonic circumstances than males other than countertenors. Where men stay primarily to exclusively in vibrational mode one, with its thicker vocal fold shape and larger vertical phase difference, women in Western classical singing transition from mode one into vibrational mode two, with its thin, stretched vocal fold shape, in their low or lower middle range. A third vibrational mode—whistle register, with stiff vocal folds that typically do not fully close—is used for extremely high pitches, above ca. C6.

Secondly, since female ranges are about an octave higher than male ranges, women have half as many harmonics within keyboard range available for resonation. (This can be dramatically demonstrated on the *Madde* synthesizer: see *Madde* Exploration 2, p. 118.) For this reason, tuning the first formant to available harmonics is much more crucial for female resonance, the higher the pitch, the more relevant the principle.

Thirdly, with vocal tracts that are on average 20% shorter than male vocal tracts, most women have fewer formants within keyboard range—often only three—from which to form their timbre. That nonetheless still covers the necessary bases of vowel formants (F1 and F2) and a possible singer's formant (F3). Once a singer is above ca. D5, the singer's formant is of decreasing importance to overall resonance and projection, since the fundamental frequency becomes the dominant harmonic and is high enough in frequency to generate the necessary loudness level.

Finally, since first formants lie in contact with the treble clef, women face the need to resort to the F1 tracking of H1 (by vowel opening) described above relatively earlier in their range than men, from ca. G4-G5. In other words, as soon as a singer reaches the pitch of the first formant of a vowel, she will need to open that vowel for any higher pitches.[11] Furthermore, some classical female singers will even close vowels somewhat, lowering F1 in order to formant track H1 for a headier timbre lower. Western classical female singing is therefore done in whoop mode a high percentage of the time. This active vowel modification will necessarily reduce the differences between vowels as they all approach the formant tuning of an /ɑ/ above the treble clef, medializing and to some extent neutralizing vowel timbre. Nonetheless, with sufficient textual and consonantal context, plus a continued clear conception of the intended vowel, some vowel differentiation and perceived intelligibility is possible surprisingly high in the range.

Middle Voice Challenge of Open Vowels

Women generally prefer close vowels, especially close front vowels, like /i/ and /e/, in the lower middle voice. This is due to the fact that the first formants of those vowels lie low enough in the treble clef to resonate effectively the fundamental frequency (H1) of pitches in that range. The first formant of /ɑ/, on the other hand, is at the top of or above the treble clef for sopranos, so that once mode one is relinquished, an /ɑ/ in the lower middle voice may weaken significantly. Various strategies can be used to strengthen this part of the range:

- strengthening the vocal folds themselves through exercising mode one. (The vocal folds are comprised primarily of the "chest voice" muscles; exercising mode one—in appropriate ways—creates more robust vocal folds.);

- finding a more complete glottal closure through the use of affect, greater vocal tract poise, deliberate linear motivation, creaky voice therapy, etc.;

- finding an intermediate, more gradated vocal fold thickness (While a binary shift in vibrational mode will probably always occur at some point, the shift needn't be completely polarized or radical in vocal fold shape change. Disciplined effort should be given to smoothing the transition as much as possible.);

---

[11] If a soft, silvery, less warm high float is desired, the singer can stay in closer articulation, allowing H1 (the pitch being sung) to rise above F1 (avoiding whoop tracking). However if this is done at loud dynamic levels, the tone will be shrill.

- deepening or modifying the /ɑ/ via tongue height/fronting to bring its first formant closer to the pitch being sung;
- finding a second formant resonation of H3;
- modifying to a vowel that clusters F1 and F2 enough to resonate the second harmonic that lies between them;
- shaping the resonator more convergently/closely.[12] The more convergently the /ɑ/ can be conceived, the more the vocal tract will assist vibrator efficiency.

Upper Middle Voice

When better function is achieved in the upper middle voice, sopranos often report a taller, narrower acoustic sensation of the tone, whose "dome" is "behind the eyes," rather than the wider, shorter, lateral, "mouthy" sensation of a "spread" tone. Sensation can be paradoxical. A fronted tongue, moderately close, convergent vowel posture, amused affect, and soft palate that feels lifted rather toward the front near the hard palate, all achieve an open throat, even though one has little awareness of the throat with this set of actions. Kinesthesia for throat space is notoriously false. (See Open Throat and Noiseless Inhalation, pp. 63-4.) These strategies appear to help establish the F1/H1 whoop timbre necessary for the upper voice as the female sings through the upper half of the treble clef into her top register. Some teachers recommend assisting this narrowing sensation with actual lip rounding on non-lip rounded vowels, though if the internal strategies listed above are done sufficiently, the external appearance of the vowel needn't be falsified.

Whoop Timbre and Beyond

Once a female has tracked F1 as high as possible through vowel opening (to ca. Bb5), she will need to raise her larynx to some degree for higher pitches to continue F1/H1 formant tracking. When F1 can be raised no further, the acoustic register makes a transition into whistle mode (**mode three**) in which F1 and F2 are brought close enough together so that H1 can be resonated between them by their clustered

---

[12] In general, having treble voices stay in close articulatory positions through the middle voice for all vowels whose F1 locations are higher improves convergence and resonance balance, if there is sufficient internal space and an open throat.

bandwidths. More research is needed in this area to explain the distinct vowel qualities that can sometimes be heard pitch by pitch in these stratospheric formant tunings. They are typically perceived as variants of mid to open vowels /o ɔ ɑ a æ/, most of whose vowel formants (F1 & F2) are relatively proximate. In some cases an extremely high pitch (H1) may be being resonated by F2.

Madde Exploration 5: whoop timbre and beyond

Examples of F1/H1 Tracking

In the recording of Richard Strauss' "Beim Schlafengehen" sung by soprano Leontyne Price (See Appendix 5: Youtube Examples: Example 1, p. 128) there are several excellent examples of F1/H1 tracking of mid-close vowels. The melisma on the word "sehnliches" demonstrates tracking in a close /e/ vowel (0:40). Notice how the

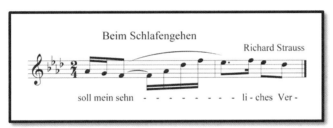

Figure 10: F1 tracking of H1 in "sehnliches": whoop timbre /e/.

singer opens the vowel to keep F1 close to the pitch being sung. Then the /ɪ/ vowel in "Kind" at 1:00 is also actively opened/modified to maintain whoop timbre. In both cases the opening of the vowel is sufficient to keep H1 within the effective bandwidth of F1 for fullness and roundness of tone quality.

Figure 11: F1 tracking of H1 in "Kind": whoop timbre /ɪ/.

A more dramatic example of maintaining whoop timbre by F1 tracking of H1 is at 2:45-3:01 on the /e/ of the word "Seele":

Figure 12: F1 tracking of H1 in "Seele": whoop timbre /e/.

Finally, at 3:18-3:30 the close vowels /y/ and /e/ in "Flügen" and "schweben" are opened significantly in order to track the resonance of an F1/H1 match.

Figure 13: F1 tracking of H1 in "Flügen" and "schweben": whoop timbre /y/ and /e/.

The fact that vowels must be opened once the sung pitch reaches the frequency of a vowel's first formant has been known for some time. Just how the vowel is to be opened—so that the larynx stays low, the throat open, and the resonator as convergent and well tuned as the circumstance allows—will need coaching and refinement in the teacher/student partnership.

(See Acoustics of Belting, p. 68, for an alternative female acoustic strategy.)

Chapter 7
Male *Passaggio* Training

To review briefly, a relatively stable tube (vocal tract) length is necessary for consistent depth and balance of timbre in Western classical singing. Both tube length and cross sectional area are responsible for formant locations. Effective tube length determines the general location of the entire formant set of a given voice, including the *Fach* specific singer's formant cluster. However, untrained males instinctively shorten the vocal tract upon ascending, raising the first formant in order to preserve the strong F1/H2 acoustic coupling of the yell, a behavior that appears to be a universal, hardwired survival trait. Yelling results in an increasingly pressed mode of phonation, a heavier (thyroarytenoid [TA] dominant) laryngeal registration adjustment, and inconsistency of timbre and perceived *Fach*. If vocal tract length and shape are kept stable, first formant locations will remain stable and the yell will be avoided by allowing H2 to pass through and above F1. This transition results in the timbral shift variously referred to as "covering" or "turning over," and facilitates an easier laryngeal registration adjustment and a less pressed mode of phonation. Knowledge of the variety of F1 locations by vowel and their predictable F1/H2 crossings when singing an octave lower, as well as the passive vowel modifications that accompany those crossings, becomes both an accurate means of assessing tube length stability and a reliable basis for developing effective strategies for training tube stability for successful *passaggio* negotiation.

Male *Passaggio* Objectives
The main technical objectives in training male transition into the upper voice are:

• A Stable Laryngeal Position and Tube Length, and a Convergent Resonator
A stable laryngeal position and tube length with a relatively convergent resonator shape ensures depth and consistency of timbre. A stable

tube length is accomplished by avoiding activation of the swallowing muscles that raise the larynx and constrict the laryngopharynx. This can be monitored by palpating the thyrohyoid space toward the back of the larynx on either side. (See figure 14 below, and Monitoring Tube Length Stability, p. 65.) It should remain loose and open. Muscularly fixing the larynx in a low position will interfere with vocal freedom. Maintaining timbral depth and degree of vowel closeness until after the vowel has turned over assists in discouraging laryngeal elevation upon pitch ascent. A convergent resonator shape—more open near the larynx and closer near the lips—facilitates the development of the singer's formant cluster and *chiaroscuro*, balanced resonance. It requires some degree of tongue fronting and elevation of the soft palate, and the least degree of jaw drop necessary for the vowel/pitch combination being sung. It should seem to the singer that inner opening "leads" and jaw opening follows, rather than vice versa.

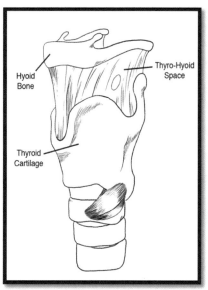

Figure 14: The thyrohyoid space

• Dynamic Laryngeal Registration
A dynamic laryngeal registration with smooth, gradual changes ensures ease and dynamic flexibility. While using appropriate resonance strategies usually improves laryngeal registration, it does not guarantee effective muscular adjustments. Dynamic (ever-changing) laryngeal registration appropriate to pitch requires some separate attention. Knowledge of the effects of vowel on resonance and registration can inform creative exercise strategies and therapies. For example smoothly gliding from a chesty open vowel to a heady close vowel an octave higher can give laryngeal muscles an opportunity to discover dynamic adjustments. Singing scalar passages in which deliberate, successively

closer vowel choices coincide with ascending pitch can also coax laryngeal adjustments toward lighter registral adjustment, and vice versa for descent. While changes in the percentages of the TA and CT involvement may be trained to be fairly gradual, acoustic feedback factors will likely precipitate a binary shift from vibrational mode one (short, thick folds, loose cover) to mode two (long, taut, thin folds, taut cover) at some point in the scale, though skillful singers are able to minimize the timbral effect of this shift. Males (other than countertenors) resort to mode two infrequently, but do need lighter adjustments of mode one for the upper range.

• Familiarity with Vowel Turning

A familiarity with the locations, sounds, and sensations of vowel turning is necessary. Since letting the voice turn over—rather than yelling—is not instinctive, knowing when and where to expect vowels to turn over can be very helpful to the young singer. If vowels do not turn over where expected, one of two things has happened to keep the first formant above the second harmonic: the vowel has been opened (a sometimes reasonable but pitch and diction limited strategy) or the larynx has been raised (rarely a good strategy), or most likely, both. Experiencing vowel turning on the close vowels /i/ and /u/ which close well below the traditional *passaggio* location can be instructive. Close /o/ and /e/ turn at about the traditionally understood location of the *primo passaggio,* at the low end of the *zona di passaggio.* Their depth and closeness are relatively easy to monitor and coach. An untrained male will tend to open /o/ toward /ʌ/ and /e/ toward /ɛ/ rather than allowing the turn. Resonant, inflective speech sounds that loop above (glide up over and back down through) the predicted pitch of turning and back are easy initial ways to explore vowel turning. If the yell instinct is stubborn, suggesting depth, thinking a slightly closer vowel and an internalizing affect or direction (sobby; in, down and out) while ascending, are often fruitful strategies. The eventual actual goal is to maintain rather than change tube shape while looping up, allowing the acoustic, passive modification that occurs with turning.

• The Ability to Turn Over

Once a student is familiar with turning and knows when and where vowels should turn over, the ability to allow vowels to turn over at appropriate pitches should be rehearsed until routine and non-manipulative. If the best resonance "posture" is being maintained, a loop up and down on any vowel will turn over and back with consistent *chiaroscuro* timbre, ease, and without a significant, inevitable crescendo toward the crest of the loop. There may also be a sense of the tone settling in an inner direction with upward inflection, and back toward the front of the hard palate when reopening upon descent.

• Vowel Integrity with Appropriate Vowel Modification

The passive vowel modification that accompanies vowel turning should not distort vowels, rather it should be in same natural vowel family or on the same side of the "front-back" street, and not interfere with intelligibility. Specifically, modifications on the "back vowel" side of the street—/ɑ ɔ ʊ o/—will move in the direction of a closer neighbor on the same side of the street. Similarly vowels on the "front" side of the street—/ɛ e ɪ/—will close somewhat and possibly slightly neutralize. Since they will already have closed much lower, the close vowels /i/ and /u/ will need to be opened toward /ɪ/ and /ʊ/—at least in degree of vertical space if not in vowel quality—in the *zona di passaggio* in order to avoid whoop timbre and stay virile and resonant. However, the mixing of back vowels such as /ɑ/ or /ɔ/ "across the street" toward /ɛ/ or toward a mixed vowel such as /œ/ is a distortion (see Vowel Modification Revisited below).

• Maintenance of *Chiaroscuro* Timbre

While the upper voice of professional male singers should have an exciting, ringing quality, there should also be timbral fullness and depth. This is accomplished by maintaining tube length and the open throated, convergent resonator poise necessary for the depth-dependent singer's formant cluster, even while the tube shape is being otherwise modified (i.e., when formants one and two are involved in some range specific formant tuning).

Vowel Modification Revisited

The question of **vowel modification** vs. **vowel integrity** or "purity" has been much debated during the history of vocal pedagogy. Both concepts require yet elude clear definition, since human perception is involved. Given the demonstrable fact that timbre changes somewhat when harmonics rise through formants, some degree of vowel modification or change is inevitable. However, vowel modification has historically ranged from conscious vocal tract shape changes with the intent of producing a modified vowel timbre to outright vowel substitution. The concept of passive vowel modification introduced here points out that some degree of vowel shift will inevitably occur when the vocal tract (tube), i.e., vowel shape, is kept stable while the pitch (with its set of harmonics) is raised, as harmonics move through the first formant. This kind of vowel change will feel to the singer like s/he is maintaining the vowel—at least in shape—while allowing a subtle migration within the same family, or on the same "side of the street" in terms of front-back designation. What all teachers presumably want to avoid is the perception of a vowel distortion. This occurs when, for example, an open back vowel, such as /ɔ/ takes on some of the quality of a mixed vowel such as /œ/. This is more indicative of tongue tension than of the acoustics of turning over, and does not result from maintaining the normal speech shape of /ɔ/ over the F1/H2 crossing, which should migrate instead in the direction of /ʊ/.

The phenomenon of passive vowel modification invites the question of what vowel modification is or should be altogether. Is it a deliberate reshaping of the resonator to that of a different speech vowel posture in the attempt to find a more favorable formant/harmonic coupling? Or is it rather a perceptual change that occurs as a result of maintaining vowel shape while changing pitch, and thus changing formant/harmonic relationships? Or is it perhaps both, depending upon the circumstance? These questions require further research, but in this author's opinion, below the turn to just above it, the latter (maintaining shape) should prevail. Between the turn and whoop timbre, either can be used. From F1/H1 whoop coupling and higher, some form of active shape change (vowel opening) must be used to

41

maintain timbral fullness, regardless of how the singer motivates that shape change. Ideally a singer should be able to continue to think the vowel of the word being sung, but with the addition of more space— primarily internal vertical space with an accompanying opening of the mandible. Some singers get a better result by actually thinking a more open neighbor vowel (vowel substitution). Subtleties of shaping will enable one to preserve the intended vowel identity more or less well relative to other vowels at the same pitch. That said, if the vocal tract shape necessary for a resonant but convincingly understandable /i/ vowel on a tenor high C (C5), is used an octave lower, it will not sound like an /i/, whether one was thinking /i/ or /ɪ/ or some other motivational modification. Conversely, if a tenor attempts a normal speech range /i/ shape on C5, the timbre—if phonation is even possible— will primarily sound strained and/or strangled. Changing the shape of the vocal tract in such situations (when singing above the normal F1 frequency) is essential, both for good sound and for vocal ease.

One principle at play in all modification has to do with the number of harmonics that lie below the first formant. The lower the pitch being sung, the more harmonics there will be below the first formant. Furthermore, when singing lower pitches, usually a higher number harmonic (H3 or higher) will be rising through the first formant, and the harmonic below it will be trailing more closely, often already well within the bandwidth (climbing the skirt) of F1. The trailing harmonic is therefore positioned to be resonated by F1 and thus able to assume the prominence just relinquished by its higher neighbor. With multiple harmonics below the first formant, there are also more closely spaced harmonics available above the first formant to be resonated by formants two and higher, hence little need to modify the shape for better formant/harmonic matches. Therefore active vowel modification—beyond a generally good, convergent acoustic poise of the vocal tract—should not be needed in the range where two or more harmonics lie below F1.

Higher harmonics (with closer trailing harmonics) rising through the first formant generate audible, but subtler timbral closings or turnings.

However, when the second harmonic rises through the first formant, the trailing first harmonic is almost an octave below, and the resultant timbral shift (not to mention the interactive feedback effect on the vibrator) is more significant. Once whoop timbre is achieved, that is, once H1 has arrived at the frequency peak of F1, no trailing harmonics remain (there are no harmonics below H1—it is by definition the lowest harmonic), and there are many fewer higher harmonics within primary color range (keyboard range) available for resonation. Therefore with higher pitch, formant tuning becomes increasingly necessary, the higher the fundamental, the more essential and greater the modification. Should the first harmonic rise *above* the first formant, since there are no harmonics below the first formant for it to resonate, the timbre will quickly thin, and formant tuning (raising F1 in tandem with the pitch being sung) becomes essential.

Non-Linear Source-Filter Theory Revisited

The purpose of active vowel modification just discussed is to adjust formants in order to find a better resonation of available source harmonics. As mentioned rather earlier, in certain circumstances acoustic energy passing through the filter can be productively reflected back onto the source, assisting the efficiency and power of the voice source/vibrator. Such interactivity can effectively increase the **closed quotient** (percentage of closure time in each vibrational cycle) of the vibrator. This makes the resonator more efficient for the upper end of the spectrum: the longer the **closed phase**, the stronger the reinforcement of higher harmonics. It also reduces airflow *without* the need for greater muscular glottal closure force (glottal squeeze). The circumstances in which interactivity is enhanced are: a more **convergent resonator** shape, a settled larynx, open throat, and narrowed exit of the **epilaryngeal tube**. All of these conditions increase acoustic **inertive reactance**, a factor that can improve glottal efficiency. These characteristics (open throat, resonator convergence) are especially typical of Western classical singing in the creation of its *chiaroscuro* (bright/dark) balanced resonance and **singer's formant cluster**. (Sundberg, 1974; Titze & Story, 1997; Titze & Verdolini, 2012)

The influence of the resonator upon the vibrator had been anticipated by earlier voice teacher/researchers such as Berton Coffin, Ralph Appleman, and John Large, and intuited by voice teachers for centuries, but the physics involved has only more recently been explained by voice science researchers such as Johan Sundberg, Ingo Titze, and Donald Miller. At present, non-linear interactivity seems to apply primarily to vocal tract strategies (a convergent resonator) present in Western classical singing and not as often used in other singing styles that employ a more divergent vocal tract shaping strategy.

Resonator Convergence

Voice scientist Ingo Titze has observed that Western classical singers use a vocal tract shape that is relatively convergent, as in an inverted megaphone, presumably in order to maximize inertive reactance for classical resonance efficiency. As explained above, the creation of the singer's formant cluster and *chiaroscuro* timbre requires a relatively convergent resonator shape. Close front vowels, given their tongue contact with the upper molars, are inherently convergent, but may still need some additional pharyngeal space (a hint of yawn or feeling of verticality behind the tongue/teeth contact). Open vowels will need some adjustment to achieve maximal convergence, within the limits of acceptable vowel intelligibility. For example, pronouncing open vowels within speech range with the least amount of jaw drop and tongue flattening—retaining as fronted a tongue as can be managed with good diction—will increase their convergence. Convergence is also dependent upon a relatively settled, open throat, in which the thyrohyoid space has not been compressed (Figure 14, p. 38), and upon some elevation of the soft palate. A convergent vocal tract poise can be more naturally achieved through the use of motivational affects, such as inner pleasure, suppressed laugh, mischief, sobbiness, etc., affects that stimulate a low larynx, open throat, lifted palate, and closer vowel postures. All such adjustments should result in better *chiaroscuro* resonance, comfortably and freely achieved.

Vocal Cover/Turning Over

If vowels turn over at their predicted locations—slightly less than an octave below the resonant speech locations of their first formants—that is evidence of tube length stability, a desirable characteristic in Western classical singing. Therefore, observing the location of vowel turnings is useful for assessing and training tube length stability. Raising the larynx with pitch ascent—due to the yell instinct—is a remarkably strong and universal response. Countering this instinct by training the larynx to float low even when ascending, constitutes a significant part of training singers, especially males. It is important for the teacher and singer to understand, respect, and allow the necessary harmonic/formant crossings that result from a stable tube length during pitch ascent, and the subtle passive vowel modifications that accompany each successive timbral closing. Furthermore, understanding the relationship between vowel closeness and first formant locations provides an effective tool for encouraging vowel turning when habit and instinct undermine tube length stability and resist vowel turning. If the tube shortening/vowel opening "yell" response is stubbornly persistent, deepening the timbre along with some degree of vowel closing can be temporarily used to precipitate turning over until the habitual response is retrained. The degree of closure can be accomplished by vowel choice or closeness of vowel pronunciation, such as insisting on a "Minnesotan" (or German closed) /o/; moving to a closer neighbor vowel: /o/ to /u/; /e/ to /ɪ/; or by physical directions that accomplish sufficient closeness, such as maintaining contact between the tongue hump and molars, making sure the soft palate is lifted, or maintaining lip or tongue shape.

Secondary Acoustic Registration Events

As mentioned above, there are audible effects whenever any harmonic crosses the first formant—closings when a harmonic rises through the first formant, and openings when a harmonic drops below the first formant. Like the primary turning of the voice when H2 rises through F1, the locations of all other harmonic/formant crossings are predictable, and therefore pedagogically useful. The third harmonic will cross a first formant when singing an octave and a fifth below the formant;

the fourth harmonic two octaves below; and so forth. Given these larger intervallic distances below first formant locations, the resultant intersections necessarily happen more often on low pitches and on open vowels, hence more often within the bass clef, or in male voices.

Handling the *Zona di Passaggio*

All of these crossings provide opportunities for inappropriate adjustments of tube length or shape (shortening and opening). This is more often an issue when ascending, since F1 tends to track rising harmonics, making timbral closing less instinctive than timbral opening. For example, the third harmonic crosses the first formant of the open vowels /ε/, /ɔ/, and /ɑ/ just below the traditional location of the *primo passaggio,* generating an audible "mini-turning" or "mini-closing" that is often described as seeming acoustically "narrower" and "taller" to the singer. If this crossing does not happen, the larynx has been raised and the vowel opened, causing the *zona di passaggio* to sound too blatant or wide open, and setting the singer up for a more difficult transition through the *secondo passaggio.* This may explain the frequently encountered "hourglass" perception or description of the *zona di passaggio* and directives to "narrow," "gather," or "collect" the voice through the *passaggio.*

Furthermore, the first formants of the close vowels /i/ and /u/ in their normal speech shapes lie in the vicinity of the *secondo passaggio,* and pitches on those vowels would have closed acoustically an octave lower, well below even the *primo passaggio.* Unless the singer wants to move into whoop coupling (F1/H1) at the *secondo passaggio,* he will need to open /i/ and /u/ through the *zona di passaggio* in order to avoid whoop timbre and stay in a more virile mixed timbre. In any case he will certainly need to open /i/ and /u/ at the *secondo passaggio* and above to avoid thinness of timbre and tightness of phonation, since in their normal speech shapes, whoop coupling (F1/H1) would have been reached by then, and—if no adjustment is made—exceeded above it. Though it is counterintuitive, due to their relative F1 locations, an /i/ in the upper voice will need to be more open than an /ɑ/ at the same pitch in order to match in registral timbre.

These secondary acoustic registration events create opportunities not only for inappropriate adjustments, but also can be exploited for training purposes. The primary acoustic transition of the F1/H2 crossing of the open vowels near the *secondo passaggio* can be reliably modeled an octave lower, where H4 crosses F1. Though the passive vowel modification is subtler at the F1/H4 interaction, it offers the advantage of rehearsing an acoustic transition similar to F1/H2 without the challenges of laryngeal registration faced an octave higher. Learning how to maintain tube shape and to allow the resultant vowel migration (passive modification) is crucial to the training of Western classical singing.

Summary of Events that Surround the Male *Zona di Passaggio*

All of the acoustic registration events that surround the male *passaggio* can be charted on the musical staff for clearer comprehension:

Bass Passaggio Events
F1/H1, F1/H2 & F1/H3 Crossings

Figure 15: The acoustic registration events that surround the *passaggio* are charted in the bass clef between the brackets: the black pitches represent the primary turning of the vowels at the F1/H2 crossings; the open vowels /ɛ/, /ɑ/, and /ɔ/ turn or close near the *secondo passaggio* and the close vowels /e/ and /o/ near the *primo passaggio;* the red pitches represent the "mini-turnings" of the F1/H3 crossings of the open vowels /ɛ/, /ɑ/, and /ɔ/ near the *primo passaggio;* and the first formant locations of /i/ and /u/—also near the *secondo passaggio*—indicate the point at which whoop timbre would occur and above which first formant tracking of H1 would be necessary. (See Appendix 3 for charts of *passaggio* events for all male voice types, p. 126.)

Primo Passaggio

(events that occur in the vicinity of the *primo passaggio*)

- the mini-turnings (F1/H3 crossings) of the open vowels /ɛ/, /ɔ/, and /ɑ/
- the primary turnings (F1/H2) of the semi-close vowels /e/ and /o/

Secondo Passaggio

(events that occur in the vicinity of the *secondo passaggio*)

- the primary turnings (F1/H2) of the open vowels /ɛ/, /ɔ/, and /ɑ/
- arrival in whoop timbre (F1/H1) of the close vowels /i/and /u/

Registration and Expression/Artistry

Along with the primary turn, these secondary timbral events are not only important for elegant range negotiation, but can also be exploited for artistic purposes, since their passive timbral modifications are often associated with expression. A male voice that "opens" further upon descending through a harmonic/formant crossing can sound richer and emotionally fuller. Conversely, the deepening and rounding of timbre that accompanies ascending timbral closures (cover) is colorful and emotionally warming and/or exciting. One can actively precipitate these effects safely—when sufficiently near their predictable locations—by subtle degrees of vowel opening or closing. The thrill of a high note can be increased by accessing the resonance boost of an F2/higher harmonic coupling upon turning over. If a soft, sweet yet full head tone effect is sought on an /i/ or an /u/ near the *secondo passaggio*, the singer can stay in close pronunciation to access full "whoop" timbre, and open gradually above that to continue to track H1 with F1. (See Effect of Approach by Leap, p. 53, and Timbral Openings and Closings Other than F1/H2, p. 56.)

Chapter 8
Perceptions of Turning Over

The reader may wonder, "When a voice turns over—when H2 rises through F1—what does it sound like to the audience? And what does it sound and feel like to the singer?"

First it should be noted that this question is significant primarily for male voices, since all vowels will have turned over in the octave below G4, and for deep voices as early as by D4. Furthermore, the answer is complicated by the fact that it will vary a bit from vowel to vowel, from voice type to voice type, and from whether the cause is active or passive vowel modification. Finally, since sensory perceptions are highly individual, predictive descriptions of perception are inherently risky and therefore cannot be foolproof. All that said, the following descriptions and pedagogic opinions—admittedly based on personal experience, anecdote, impression, and student response, but not subjected to rigorous testing—are typical and may prove useful.

Perception of Vowel and Timbre
When well executed, the timbral change and passive modification asso-ciated with turning over is usually subtle. If vowels are divided into front and back "families" or sequences, /i ɪ e ɛ æ a/ and /u o ʊ ɔ ɑ/,[13] listed from closest to most open, then the passive modification of the vowel will be in the same vowel family or sequence. The more open back or rounded vowels move toward a closer neighbor: /ɔ/ will move toward /ʊ/; /o/ toward /ʊ/ or /u/. The more open front vowels close slightly and may also medialize or neutralize somewhat: /ɛ/ will seem to migrate in the direction of /e/ or /ɪ/ with a possible hint of /œ/, but with no change of lip shape. Indeed, if these are truly passive modifications, *no shape change* in the direction of those vowel migrations should be made. The original vowel and vocal tract shape should be deliberately maintained through the turn. In particular,

---

[13] The relative closeness of /ʊ/ and /o/ are debatable, and depend upon pronuncia-tion. In this author's experience, the F1 of resonant /ʊ/ is higher, making it more open.

while care should be taken to keep the laryngopharyngeal depth factor stable (the open-throated, settled larynx), aspects of the vocal tract shape that are toned and tuned for perceptual "height" and "ring" should be emphasized to avoid excessive dulling of the timbre across the turn. The student may be tempted to move toward excessive orality (yell response), or to modify the vowel heavily (by tube lengthening, and closing the vowel shape), or simply to collapse the shape toward neutrality ("anonymous vowel"), all of which should be avoided. When well produced, the timbral shift will feel acoustic, not muscular, and even the change in acoustic sensation will be subtle, not heavy.

Perception of Tonal Sensation

The very term "turning over" is descriptive of the acoustic sensation. There is a sense of the top of the tonal sensation arching, tipping or rolling up and over into the head and toward the front, i.e., turning over, and reverberating around in the head more as opposed to coming directly out of the mouth as in open timbre. At the same time there may be an opposite sensation of the "underbelly" of the tone settling into the body and rolling down and under. This latter aspect counters the reaching up and out sensation typical of the yell. Together these sensations might seem like the two ends of a scroll rolling up and over toward the front, and down and under into the body. The "back wall" of an open throated tonal sensation should neither be moved forward nor moved further back through the turn. There is also the sense that the tone is increasingly settled and open in the torso, acoustically collected, and convergent or narrowing to the front, rather than widening.

Unless whoop timbre is desired, passive modification will not suffice for the two closest vowels, /i/ and /u/, which will have closed already well below the *passaggio*. They will need to be actively opened through the male *zona di passaggio* to retain a virile quality and continue to open with further ascent. In general, when opening a vowel, the vertical stretching of its internal dimension should seem to lead the opening. The jaw opening should follow rather than lead, and feel more like settling in, back and down than like reaching out and down.

Perception by Voice Type and Vowel

The lighter the male voice type, usually the lighter the turn and modification will sound. The lower, heavier, or deeper the voice type, the more noticeable the turn will likely sound. *Leggiero* tenors may have rather subtle timbral shifts, while basses, deep baritones, and dramatic tenors tend to have more obvious, even dramatic shifts. The turn is also more obvious on open vowels, especially open back vowels such as /ɔ/ and /ɑ/. The stronger the ring component of a vowel through the turn—if freely gotten—the better the turn, and the less "covered" the resultant tone. This may be due to a sufficiently strong singer's formant or to an effective second formant/higher harmonic coupling above the turn.

Difference in Effect Between Active and Passive Modification

In scalar passages it is most elegant to accomplish a smooth, gradual turning across the span of a couple of pitches. However, the turn can be exaggerated in any voice by active vowel modification: choosing a more open timbre just below the turn, then creating a deliberate, heavier cover at the turn, especially if coordinated with a shift to F2 prominence on a higher harmonic. Specifically this involves initially opening the timbre, postponing the turn, then subsequently lowering F1 by closing the vowel shape and/or lengthening the vocal tract. Such a move will precipitate a more dramatic, deliberate turn, which— if not too exaggerated—might be effective for strong expressive effect, but should be reserved for special circumstances. Multiple examples of such a use can be heard in tenor Nicolai Gedda's recording of the Rachmaninoff *Vocalise* (See Appendix 5: Youtube Examples: Example 2, p. 128). Whether or not using this strategy to this extent is ideal in this song is debatable. In this recording Gedda tends not to smooth the transition from open to close. Instead he often sings deliberately open timbres just below the turn, and then overtly "hooks" into the turn. For example, about three minutes into the *Vocalise*, Gedda chooses to sing an E4 to F#4 from rather open to close timbre, then immediately afterwards sings the F#4 in open timbre, closing only as he moves to G#4 (figure 16). A skillful singer does have some latitude in having the turn occur at slightly different pitches on the same vowel—within narrow pitch limits. If the pitch of turning is moved away

Figure 16: Rachmaninoff *Vocalize* excerpt, mm. 26-29

from its normal location, it is usually delayed to a higher pitch (via opening) for loud dynamic levels, or done at lower pitches (via closing) as a strategy to soften the dynamic. An /ɑ/ vowel held in open timbre higher than its normal turning location will sound a bit spread and blatant, as it does in a few instances in this recording of Gedda on some open F#4's. That said, Gedda's excellent, smooth laryngeal registration shift to mode two in the final ascent to C#5 is unequaled.

Perception of Turning in a Deeper Voice

Excellent examples of the more obvious turn typical of deeper voices can be found in Ravel's *Kaddish* recorded by José Van Dam. In the long melismatic passage on /ɑ/ near the end of the piece, Van Dam's voice turns over where expected. The vowel shift is rather notable in this rich, deep, beautiful voice, but is typical for such voice types. (See Appendix 5: Youtube Examples: Example 3, ca. 3:48)

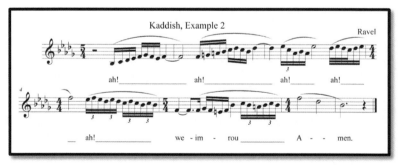

Figure 17: Ravel *Kaddish* excerpt, mm. 46-53.

Effect of Approach by Leap

The turn of the voice can be especially exciting when approached by leap from below, since the inherent color change from open to close timbre is placed in sharper distinction by the leap, even when smoothly done. Many examples of the drama and thrill of the turn of the voice in exciting top tones can be found. For example, Jussi Bjoerling's recordings (video with orchestra, audio with piano) of *"Ah, Love, but a day!"* by Amy Beach has several clear and compelling examples. (See Appendix 5: Youtube Examples: Example 4) In the very first statement of the text, "Ah, Love, but a day," both the /ʌ/ of "love" on F4 and the /ɛːi/ in his pronunciation of "day" on Eb4 are in open timbre. This provides a clear comparison to the second statement of the same text, in which both vowels turn over: the /ʌ/ of "love" on Ab4 and /ɛːi/ of "day" on G4. Furthermore, the second occurrence of "day," after starting in close timbre on G4, opens during the *portamento* down a major third to Eb4 (figure 18). Later in this same phrase, the word "world" also starts in close on F4 and then opens with the downward *portamento* to B3. A later example of how vowels vary from close to

Figure 18: Beach *Ah, Love, but a day!* excerpt, mm. 2-9.

open timbre in the same general tessitura occurs midway through the song at the first entry of "Look in my eyes" (See figure 19). "Look" on the vowel /ʊ/ on F4 is in close timbre, and the /ɑ/ of "eyes" shortly afterwards, though only a half step lower, is in open timbre. The second entry of this text begins similarly, but this time the /ɑ/ of "eyes" begins in open timbre on Eb4, then dramatically moves to close timbre in the leap up to the Ab4—G4. This continues with a close timbre /ɪ/ in "Wilt" on F4, and an open /ɑ/ in "thou" on E4 that then closes on the step up to F4 in the orchestral recording, but not in the piano recording.

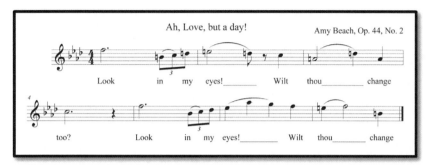

Figure 19: Beach *Ah! Love, but a day!* excerpt, mm. 26-32.

While these timbral shifts are smoothly accomplished, they are none-theless quite evident, and become part of the expressive inflection of Bjoerling's beautiful voice. They are primarily passive acoustic events that result from his retaining a vowel shape across the pitch of turning for that vowel.

Darkened Timbre

When depth is maintained during ascent, the singer may perceive the timbre as more vertical and possibly even somewhat darkened (see Cover Terminology, p. 74). A second recording of Bjoerling in a live performance of Handel's "Ombra mai fù" demonstrates a deliberately "darkened timbre" which augments the effects of turning as in a deeper voice type, creating a rather dramatic effect (See Appendix 5: Youtube Examples: Example 5). If one lays aside questions of Baroque style by today's standards, this is a rather remarkable demonstration of vocalism and of timbral openings and closings. For example, Bjoerling begins the opening /o/ on D4 of "Ombra" at 1:52 in close timbre and then crescendos to open timbre on /ɔ/.

Figure 20: Close to open on the same note and vowel.

Later at 2:18, the /ɑ/ vowels in the ascending "cara ed a<u>ma</u>bile" go from open timbre on E4 and F#4 to dramatically close timbre on G4.

Figure 21: Dramatic stepwise turn on /ɑ/.

In the subsequent setting of the same text at 2:45-52, /ɑ/ is kept in open (or mini-turned) timbre while /ɛ/ is close at about the same pitches.

Figure 22: Comparison of /ɑ/ and /ɛ/.

The /u/ of "fù" is close on B3 at 3:10. The high "<u>di vegeta</u>bile" begins predictably in close timbre, then opens on the E4 /ɑ/.

Figure 23: /ɑ/ from close to open.

The final high "soave più" closes on the F#4 "-ve" and stays in close timbre on G4 "più." Although remaining in close timbre, the articulation of "più" is opened in order to be more robust. Staying in close articulation when the sung pitch approaches F1 of a vowel will result in whoop timbre—too "heady" for this climactic moment. The mouth and jaw are instead opened to that of a tall /ʊ/. Finally, the final /u/ of "più" on G3 at 3:49 is an example of a normally close vowel in open timbre for greater intensity.

Figure 24: Comparison of high, close, yet robust /u/ with low open /u/.

Timbral Openings and Closings Other than F1/H2

Lower timbral closings and openings, such as those that occur at the F1/H3 and even F1/H4 junctures, can often be clearly heard as well. Earlier in the recording cited above of Ravel's *Kaddish* sung by José Van Dam (See Appendix 5: Youtube Examples: Example 3), the mini-turn of the F1/H3 crossing can be heard when Van Dam sings a melisma (at one minute into the recording) on /ɑ/ as it rises from F3 to Bb3. The mini-turn happens at Ab3, about a fifth below the primary turn of /ɑ/ (figure 25).

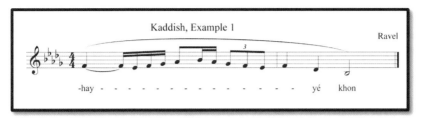

Figure 25: Ravel *Kaddish* excerpt, mm. 13-14.

Several excellent examples of F1/H2, F1/H3, and F1/H4 crossings can be heard in bass-baritone George London's recording of Schubert's "An die Musik" (See Appendix 5: Youtube Examples: Example 6). For example, the *portamento* on "wieviel" at 0:14 from G#3 to B2 demonstrates the primary F1/H2 opening of the close vowel /i/.

Figure 26: *portamento* from close to open timbre on /i/.

At "wo mich des Lebens wilder Kreis" the singer goes from a close /ɪ/ on G#3 at "mich" to an open /e/ on A#2 at "Lebens" and an open /ɪ/ at "wilder."

Figure 27: from close /ɪ/ to open /e/ and /ɪ/.

At 0:56 the /ɛ/ of "bessre" on B3 is mini-turned (H3 is above F1) and the /ɛ/ of "Welt" on D#4 at 0:58 is in close timbre (H2 is above F1). The following melismas of /ɛ/ on "bessre" (B3-D#3) and "Welt" (F#3-A#2) demonstrate the H3 opening and the H4 opening respectively, since London's primary pitch of turning for /ɛ/ is C4.

Figure 28: open /ɛ/ to close /ɛ/; mini-turned /ɛ/ to very open /ɛ/.

At 2:19 the strategy of keeping /i/ and /y/ in close articulation is used to generate a soft head tone effect (approaching whoop timbre). Then the final descending *portamenti* on "Kunst" and "danke" demonstrate the F1/H2 opening of close /ʊ/ and the F1/H4 opening of /ɑ/.

Figure 29: close, heady /ɪ/ and /y/; then opening /ʊ/ and /ɑ/ on downward leaps.

For additional aural examples of these acoustic registration events, approximate sounds of vowel openings and closings can be demonstrated by voice type and vowel using the *Madde* synthesizer, if one knows how to model type and vowel with appropriate formant settings. (See *Madde* Explorations 3 and 4, pp. 119-20 and Further *Madde* Explorations, pp. 123-24..)

Chapter 9
Pedagogic Implications of Tube Acoustics

Since the vocal tract is in essence a tube resonator with natural resonances that vary by tube shape (i.e., that vary by vowel), then the following principles and strategies can form a reliable basis for a coherent, practical acoustic pedagogy.

General Principles

- In seeking harmonic/formant matches, singers are not really free to tune their harmonics. Harmonics automatically result from and are built upon the fundamental frequency (pitch) they are asked by the composer to sing. Singers do have some ability to shape the vocal tract to retune the formants that selectively resonate those harmonics—especially F1 and F2.
- There are four possible formant/harmonic interactions:
    - A formant can allow a moving harmonic to pass through it.
    - A formant can be tuned to move across a stable harmonic.
    - A formant can be tuned to track a harmonic.
    - A formant can be "detuned" away from a harmonic.
- All acoustic registration events occur relative to the first formant location of each vowel. (The second formant is also often involved.)
- Laryngeal registration adjustments are sometimes independent of acoustic registration events, but are also often influenced by interactivity with acoustic registration phenomena.
- There is an audible event whenever any harmonic crosses the first formant: a timbral closing when a harmonic rises through F1, and a timbral opening when a harmonic drops below F1.
- If tube length and shape are kept the same, the vowel and timbre will increasingly close with ascending pitch and increasingly open with descending pitch.
- A voice does not turn over at the same pitch for all vowels.

- Each vowel will turn over just above an octave below its first formant, where the H2 of the pitch being sung rises above the vowel's first formant.
- Other mini-closings or openings—involving higher harmonics intersecting F1—should also occur at locations that are predictable by vowel, pitch, and vocal *Fach*.
- Predictable, stable turning/crossing locations indicate a stable tube length and shape.
- There are only two ways to raise the first formant:
    - tube shortening
    - vowel opening
- There are only two ways to lower the first formant:
    - tube lengthening
    - vowel closing
- Changes in tube length are rarely an appropriate strategy in Western classical technique, except for the extreme high treble register.
- Exercises that explore the shifts of harmonic/formant crossings assist students in sorting out:
    - what can stay the same across range and vowel
    - what must change across range and vowel
- Awareness of first formant locations and of the characteristics of formant/harmonic interactions can form the basis for creative, effective strategies:
    - for basic range development
    - for range or registration challenges that arise within repertoire

Acoustic Strategies Across Range
- As long as the pitch being sung is low enough, that is, an octave or more below the first formant of the vowel being sung, there are enough harmonics available for resonation by the vocal tract formants to preclude the need for significant formant tuning beyond assuming a generally resonant posture (an open throat, lifted palate, fronted tongue, i.e., adjusted for convergent, singer's formant/*chiaroscuro* timbre).

- For Western classical timbre, all harmonics other than H1 should be allowed to pass through F1, i.e., without formant tracking. This takes training, since it is instinctive for F1 to track rising harmonics, especially H2 (yell timbre) and H1 (whoop timbre).

- For musical theater belt and many world music styles, F1 should track H2—as in the yell—but at healthy breath pressure and airflow levels.

- Below the primary transition (the F1/H2 crossing), stay relatively close in pronunciation, keeping the first formant comfortably low for the vowel being sung.

- Allow H2 to rise above F1 at the first formant's normal resonant speech location, causing the primary acoustic transition of "turning over" at that point.

- Above the F1/H2 crossing into close timbre, if the vocal tract length and/or vowel closeness are increased, F1 will be lowered further and the voice will move into whoop timbre earlier (lower), i.e., in well less than an octave. This is a strategy typical of some women and treble male voices, who prefer the more "head-dominant" timbre of Western classical singing.

- Above the F1/H2 crossing into close timbre, if the vocal tract length and closeness are maintained, the timbre will become increasingly close until full whoop timbre is reached at the F1/H1 juncture. This is also a strategy typical of female and treble male voices, which prefer the more "head-dominant" timbre of Western classical singing.

- Above the F1/H2 crossing into close timbre, if the vowel is gradually opened *within* close timbre, that is, not so much as to allow F1 to overtake H2, whoop timbre can be postponed or even avoided altogether, and more of a "chest mix" timbre will be maintained. This is the typical strategy of men, who prefer a more virile upper voice, unless seeking a heady, softer effect. This is especially needed on those close vowels whose F1 locations are within male range.

- At the F1/H1 coupling, full whoop timbre (very heady/ falsetto) is achieved, very typical and desirable for female (or treble male) Western classical singing.

- When in whoop (F1/H1 dominant) timbre, if F2 is close to a higher harmonic, the timbre will be brighter, and possibly shrill, depending upon how much the higher harmonic is reinforced. In that situation, detuning F2 (moving it further away from the harmonic—usually lower) by active vowel modification will increase the timbral warmth and roundness.

- Above the F1/H1 (whoop timbre) juncture, the first formant must be raised in tandem with the rising fundamental (H1) in order to maintain timbral fullness or avoid thinning. This is accomplished primarily by vowel opening, but eventually by tube shortening in the extreme upper range of female or treble singing (ca. B5 and above).

- An alternative strategy for treble voices above the F1/H1 (whoop timbre) juncture might be to allow H1 (the sung pitch) to rise above F1 by retaining a closer vowel articulation, if a high soft tone with less warmth but more sparkle (a silvery, but thinner "float" quality) is sought. At loud dynamic levels this strategy would result in a shrill tone.

- When F1 can be raised no further, ending F1 tracking of the sung pitch, higher pitches will be in whistle register, being resonated by a clustering of F1 and F2.

Chapter 10
Pedagogic Strategies that Encourage Tube Stability and a Convergent Resonator

The Open Throat

A vocal tract poised for resonance (*chiaroscuro,* singer's formant timbre) should be prepared prior to singing by means of a relatively open throat and tube convergence. However, finding this pre-phonatory posture is challenging to students since our kinesthesia for throat shape is quite misleading. Most people perceive /ɑ/ to be the most open throated vowel posture and /i/ to be the least open throated, when the opposite is in fact the case (see Figure 30).

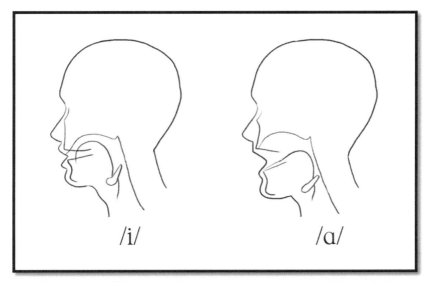

/i/   /ɑ/

Figure 30: Side view of the vocal tract shape of /i/ and /ɑ/. Paradoxical to one's kinesthesia, /i/ is open throated and /ɑ/ is fairly closed throated.

Several strategies can circumvent this false kinesthesia: a noiseless in-halation, a relatively low F1 frequency, an accurate remapping of the throat and tongue, articulatory efficiency, and the use of appropriate motivational affects.

Noiseless Inhalation

A noiseless inhalation is evidence of an open throat. It can be accomplished by a subtle palatal lift (felt more frontally, toward the hard palate) accompanied by inhaling in such a way that the teeth and front of the mouth are cooled rather than the throat. Wherever the vocal tract is the coolest, it is the narrowest, since that is where air speed will be the quickest and the resultant wind chill effect the strongest. Shaping the mouth and throat so that the cooling is in the front of the mouth causes the throat to be more open and the resonator more convergent.

Lowering the First Formant Frequency

A second strategy to achieve a convergent resonator for a noiseless inhalation is to shape the mouth and throat in a way that lowers the "pitch" of any inhalatory noise until it is inaudible. High frequency inhalatory noise highlights the F2 location, indicating a narrowed throat as is typical in whispering. Lowering the "pitch" of inhalatory noise opens the throat and highlights the F1 location instead.

Remapping the Throat and Tongue

When making the false open throated sensation of the "yawny" /ɑ/, the location of the back throat wall seems to be behind (and below) the ears, an anatomical impossibility. What is most likely being felt are those lateral tongue muscles (styloglossus) that attach to the styloid processes beneath the ears and retract the tongue toward the back throat wall. Remapping the throat wall to its actual location in front of (and below) the ears releases tongue retraction, allowing a more fronted tongue and more throat space. Furthermore, many singers map the tongue like an inverted "L" that descends vertically down to the larynx. Although there are some lateral muscle attachments below to the hyoid bone (hyoglossus), the largest portion of the tongue

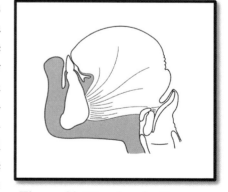

Figure 31: Mapping the Tongue

muscle, forming its body—the genioglossus—loops back under the tongue blade and attaches to the inside back of the chin. Remapping the tongue in this way creates more independence of tongue and larynx and releases the tongue for greater height and fronting. (see Figure 31.)

Monitoring Tube Length Stability

As explained above, the effect of laryngeal position on tube length stability can be monitored—in students whose anatomy lends itself to easy identification of laryngeal structure—by gently palpating the thyrohyoid space (see Figure 14, p. 38). The thyrohyoid space should be loose and open and not rise or become smaller (as it does in swallowing) with pitch ascent. Though this space varies in size between individuals, it may also have been reduced in size by residual tension from unnecessary, habitual activation of swallowing muscles during speech production. If such behavior is entrenched, it should be patiently but persistently countered and broken, preferably through therapy with a licensed speech language pathologist familiar with appropriate therapies. Effective strategies include massage and stretching of the thyrohyoid space, monitoring of the looseness and openness of the thyrohyoid space during speech production, and vocalizing with a low larynx and an extended or "rolled" tongue position. Secondly, tube length stability can be assessed by *visually* monitoring the location of the Adam's apple. This method is more useful for males, due to their larger average laryngeal anatomy, and for those with less fleshy, trimmer necks in which structures are more easily visible. Finally, tube length stability can be assessed by *aurally* monitoring the consistency of timbral depth. This is less reliable, since it can be falsely mimicked by various articulatory manipulations of tongue and lips, but careful listening and observation can reduce this liability.

Efficiency of Articulation

Another strategy for maintaining a convergent resonator while singing is to minimize the jawing of diction, reducing excessive orality. Neither vocal resonance, nor vowel articulation, nor vowel differentiation require exaggerated jaw drop or excessive articulatory change in the lower and middle range, as long as there is sufficient internal space.

On the contrary, vowels can seem fairly close to each other in formation. All of these strategies improve throat openness and lower F1, increasing resonator convergence.

Use of Affect to Position and Stabilize the Resonator

A completely lax vocal structure is vulnerable to sudden changes of pressure or situation and is therefore incompatible with optimal resonance, extremes of dynamic and range, and control of expressive timbral variety. Affect can position and stabilize the vocal apparatus more effectively than direct physical manipulation. Specific, ample and sincere expressions are typically accompanied by poised, toned vocal tract configurations which are physically stable but which stop short of muscular manipulation or rigidity. Early Italian pedagogues maintained that inhaling "through a smile" opened the throat. This is more a matter of the internal, pharyngeal poise of a genuine, deep smile than about lip shape. More recently a number of these affective positionings of the vocal tract have been tested and documented by voice teacher/researcher Jo Estill and reported by Kimberly Steinhauer (2008). For example, a suppressed laugh can stimulate retraction of the false vocal folds, reducing the possibility of pressed phonation. Strong amusement or mischief can lift and stabilize the soft palate.

Tonal "Placement" Sensations

Any discussion about tonal "placement" sensation is risky at best, since placement of sound is an illusion in the first place, and perception of tonal sensations is variable from individual to individual in the second place. Furthermore, tonal sensation is comprised of various components, probably due to a voice having multiple formants, and attention can be drawn to any one aspect of a tone's overall sensation. Finally, the harmonic content (number and spacing of harmonics) of low-pitched sounds is dramatically different than that of high-pitched sounds, generating changes of sensation across range. It is therefore prudent to proceed with caution and flexibility when suggesting tonal "placement" sensations. Nonetheless, there is potential acoustic basis for locations of tonal sensations. Consider the differences in acoustic sensation between yelling (H2 dominant, with strong upper **partials**) and whooping (H1 dominant, with weaker upper partials). Strong high partials are more likely to generate high, possibly frontal vibratory feedback to the singer, since small cavities, such as the skull bone and sinuses contain, vibrate sympathetically with high frequencies. First formant/fundamental frequency-dominant sounds are likely to be felt more centrally in the pharyngeal column, since low frequencies set larger spaces in vibration.

Second Formant "Placement" Sensations

In this regard, front and back vowel placement sensations are paradoxical. One might assume that front vowels are felt in the front and back vowels in the back. Curiously, almost the opposite is the case (see Figure 32). This is most likely due to the locations of the pressure nodes of the standing waveform of each vowel's second formant, which is predominantly felt in the oral cavity. Within a balanced over-all sensation, noticing or anticipating the acoustic energy of the second formant—for speech range pitches at least—according to the locations

mapped below, can help keep vowels "aligned," the tongue fronted, the larynx and first formant low, the resonator convergent, and the timbre balanced or *chiaroscuro*. This is more evident in male range, since pitches below ca. A4 have more harmonics within range of the second formant for resonation. At higher pitches and with appropriate vowel modification (vowel opening), tonal sensations become increasingly vertical and centralized in the head.

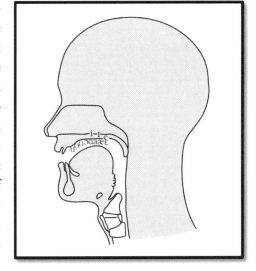

Figure 32: Resonance energy sensation locations of F2 in speech articulation. (Vowel articulation shapes are not represented in this illustration.)

Chapter 11
The Acoustics of Belting

Increasingly over the last twenty years or so, across the change of the millennium, voice teachers trained primarily or exclusively in Western classical singing have been called upon to address a wider variety of singing styles. While this text is focused on the acoustics of Western classical singing practice, one dominant, alternative muscular and acoustic strategy appears to be the basis—or at least a significant part—of many other styles of singing. That vocal style, referred to in musical theater circles as belting, will be briefly addressed below.

Research and conclusions about belting are still evolving. As of this publication, the dominant paradigm observes that belting, acoustically speaking, is a skillful form of what we have here defined as the yell: a strong F1 tracking of H2 above the normal frequency of F1 for the vowel(s) in question. It is no surprise that this mode of phonation is a very common strategy in popular music, world music, as well as in musical theater. Its unskillful form—yelling—is universal among humans. It is powerful, usually clear, high in energy, expressive, and emotionally strong. Because of its higher energy and potentially higher pressure levels, it also poses higher health risks if unskillfully executed. Yet it is also apparent that those singers who master the skills necessary to this form of vocalism manage to sustain long and healthy careers.

Let's first review the acoustic characteristics of the raw yell:

Yell Characteristics Reviewed:
Yell timbre and function is accomplished by raising the first formant through:

1) tube shortening (larynx raising),
2) pharynx narrowing, and
3) mouth widening;
4) i.e., by creating a **divergent** resonator shape.

The first two of these maneuvers are normally accomplished by activating swallowing muscles which raise and constrict the laryngo-pharynx, narrowing the throat, preventing the use of singer's formant *chiaroscuro* timbre and influencing the vibrator function toward pressed phonation.

Furthermore, yelling is typically done on open vowels like /ɑ/or/ɛ/, because their high F1 locations and inherently divergent shapes make them more compatible with the acoustic requirements of the yell. The yell is necessarily chest register (TA) or **mode one** dominant.

Belting: The *Skillful* Yell or Call

(see Semantic Differences/Belting and Yelling , p. 80.)

Which characteristics of yelling are necessary for belting and which modifications of raw yelling are needed for skillful belting? The issue is in large part how to accomplish the acoustic effect of yelling at breath pressure, breath flow, and glottal resistance levels that are sustainable and healthy.

At present, there seems to be general agreement on the following principles:

1) belting is speech-like in quality.
2) belting calls for an essentially divergent vocal tract strategy.
3) therefore, the three characteristics of yelling listed above seem necessary to some degree (raised larynx, narrowed pharynx, widened mouth),
4) vibrational mode one is extended higher—than in classical female singing at least—but may be achieved with a somewhat thinner vocal fold shape (still thicker than mode two, but somewhat less thick—referred to by some as "mix" when sufficiently high), that retains most of the timbre of "chest" but with less heft, sheer breath force, and airflow.
5) belt only really commences above the normal F1/H2 intersections, especially of the mid to open vowels, where the possibility of yelling would also start. In other words, belt is primarily in open timbre, but not all open timbre is in belt mode.

Point three is necessary in order to achieve and maintain F1 tracking of H2. However, in order to reduce the breath pressure, and especially the glottal resistance, to sustainable levels:

1) the degree of larynx raising and pharynx narrowing is probably modified somewhat (some belt teachers even maintain that while the larynx is not lowered for belt, raising the larynx is not necessary);

2) contraction/adduction of the false vocal folds is somehow inhibited (by means of strategies such as "suppressed laugh" affect (Estill));

3) breath flow is significantly reduced;

4) the aryepiglottic sphincter is significantly narrowed to achieve ring or "twang," (a brassy quality created by stronger high harmonics and a strong high formant component analogous to the singer's formant cluster of classical sound, but without the complementary depth). This strategy improves efficiency: more acoustic output for less pressure input.

Among specialists in belt, strategies are employed that:

1) achieve clean, firm, sustainable glottal closure throughout the range,

2) maximize ring/twang within the limits of the character being portrayed,

3) extend a bright, speech-like vowel shaping and quality across the entire range, sacrificing the depth and roundness of Western classical timbre to this brighter aesthetic. It might be termed *chiarochiaro* (bright/bright) timbre, in comparison to the *chiaroscuro* (bright/dark) timbre of classical singing.

4) though the resultant sound moves in the direction of pressed phonation, and may sound pressed to ears accustomed to Western classical timbre, the actual function can be accomplished by acoustic strategies that emphasize upper partials and formants, coupled with a level of glottal closure that is clean and strong but is nonetheless comfortable, sustainable, and not abusive.

Muscular Factors in Belting
There are muscular or biomechanical factors involving the vocal folds, the vocal tract, and breath management that accompany the skillful, sustainable belt.

Vocal Fold Factors
As mentioned above, the thicker vocal fold shape of vibrational mode one (chest) is maintained into the upper voice of men and extended through the middle voice of women. Opinions vary as to just how far women can extend this mode, but range at least to C5, if not higher. Individuals will certainly vary in achievable ability. However, one respected source reports that Broadway casters typically post the following expectations: "Must belt to D, must mix to F, must sing legit to A." (Lovetri, 2012).

Mix
The question of "mix" is controversial. There is actually no separate register for mix, if by register we mean a discrete laryngeal muscular function with its own distinct timbre. Many teachers—and Broadway casting agents—nonetheless use the term. What is probably meant by most for the term "mix" is:

1) an area of cooperation between the shortening, thickening thyroarytenoids and the stretching, thinning cricothyroids; that nonetheless
2) stays essentially in mode one (and retains its basic timbre); but
3) with a moderated thickness; and
4) an acoustic strategy that enables sustainably lower pressure levels.

A more recent investigation reports observing an acoustic strategy for extending yell timbre: the clustering of F1 and F2 to continue H2 dominance in the timbre, even after it has surpassed F1. If F1 and F2 are sufficiently proximate, harmonics between them—in this case H2—can still be strongly resonated. (Donald Miller 2013)

Vocal Tract Factors

In addition to the generally more divergent vocal tract shape, most belt specialists would agree on the need for a relatively poised, stabilized vocal tract, toned and tuned for maximal ring. This would involve:

1) a firmed, lifted soft palate, done in such a way as not to darken or close the timbre, rather in a way that increases ring;

2) a narrowed aryepiglottic sphincter to maximize twang/upper harmonics;

3) avoidance of false vocal fold compression, which would introduce a noise element and require higher, less sustainable breath pressure levels

4) more lateral lip opening than is typical for Western classical timbre.

All of these shaping, positioning factors should be accomplished as comfortably as possible. The muscles involved in shaping will not be lax, but should not be felt to be tight. Safe motivations for such positioning include various strong affects that stimulate the desired response. When the optimal tuning of the resonator is achieved, the sounds produced will have maximal vocal fold comfort and minimal airflow.

Breath Management Factors

While sharing the characteristics of good function common to other styles, breath management for belting does call for especially high energization, lower airflow, and somewhat higher pressure levels. Although active contraction of the thorax (bearing down in a **Valsalva maneuver**) to achieve these differences is not recommended, there may well be an awareness of greater abdominal contraction. Excess thoracic compression can be avoided by stabilizing the ribcage to some degree. For example, the muscles that pull the shoulders down and out to the sides are attached to and expand the ribs, inhibiting their downward and inward compression, as can the external intercostal muscles. Motivating this upper chest expansion with an affective stimulus (such as excitement) can reduce the risk of counterproductive rigidity. A sense of whole body involvement and full but unforced

72

commitment to expression will help distribute the extra work that the high energy levels of belting require. The singer should not perceive the higher pressure levels to be localized just below the vocal folds, rather should have a sense of a higher energy involvement of the entire body that is best organized by sincere expression.

Chapter 12
Semantic Differences

It is an understatement to observe that there has always been variety of vocal pedagogic opinion and terminology. To be sure, a teacher's choice of words—given the variety of possible attendant associations and implications—can have significant pedagogic ramifications. This leads to inevitable semantic differences and disagreements. However, the extent of disagreement may well be reduced by honest, open dialogue and a clearer definition of terms. Several such controverted terms will be discussed below for the sake of clarity and good will.

Cover Terminology

As has been pointed out earlier, the primary turn of the voice at the F1/H2 crossing is associated with the historic terms vocal *cover* and *covered*. This nomenclature unfortunately has significant baggage and does not mean the same thing to all teachers or past great singers. In a public master class Italian tenor Luciano Pavarotti demonstrated and used the term cover—in the opinion of this author—for the same phenomenon that this text refers to as the subtle *passive* vowel modification that accompanies a well executed, resonant turn of the voice. (See Appendix 5: Youtube Examples: Example 7, p. 129.) Furthermore, in another interview, Pavarotti described cover as closing, a darker timbre, and more elegant (See Youtube Examples: Example 8); and finally in a third interview went as far as to claim that if you do not cover, you are "not a real tenor" (See Youtube Examples: Example 9). Spanish tenor Alfredo Kraus maintained that he didn't believe in cover, and though his timbre was in general on the bright and at times open side, his voice did in fact turn over at or near predictable locations. There are many such variant views and uses of terms to be found, expressed by people that nonetheless seem to sing and/or teach successfully.

Some prefer to eliminate or at least reduce any awareness of the *passaggio* or *passaggio* events. Indeed, when well executed, sensations accompanying the turn will usually seem subtle and acoustic rather than muscular, enabling an ease of production. Others, such as

74

American tenor Rockwell Blake (in a public master class), described the *zona di passaggio*—as Garcia did—as a matter of "adding dark timbre" in order to preserve an adult sound (See Appendix 5: Youtube Examples: Example 10). It is fairly easy to appreciate that an open yell will sound younger, less elegant, immature, higher and more strained in timbre. Allowing the F1/H2 turn adds or retains depth and color and may indeed seem darker in timbre to the singer, but need not sacrifice ring to any great extent for the audience, and can enhance a different sort of ring than that of the yell.

Connecting Terms with Acoustic Strategies

Just below the point of the F1/H2 crossing there are at least three possible strategies that parallel the three strategies listed earlier just above the turn (see Resonance Strategies between Turning and Whoop, p. 27):

1) F1 could be actively lowered to precipitate the turn earlier/lower. It is precisely this type of ***heavy* cover**—accompanied by a more dramatic darkening and modification of the vowel—which many find objectionable. Unfortunately this strategy is equated for some teachers and singers with the very definition of cover. The physical correlates to this approach include a closer vowel pronunciation, a lowered larynx, and rounded or even trumpeted (extended) lips—in others words, active tube lengthening and vowel closing.

2) F1 could be deliberately maintained, allowing the passive modification that occurs as H2 slips above F1. This is what the term cover means in this text. The vowel is allowed to migrate smoothly to a slightly closer neighbor by means of pitch change, not shape change. The original vocal tract and vowel shape is in fact deliberately maintained through the *passaggio,* while the vowel quality is allowed to migrate subtly. With this approach it is important not to collapse the palate or vowel shape at all, not to "give in" to the vowel modification with shape changes, nor to form the speech shape of the resultant

modification or a more neutral vowel (unless a more dramatic turn is desired).

3) F1 could be either deliberately or instinctively raised by vowel opening, extending open timbre upward and delaying the turn of the voice. This can only be done well if diction allows and just for a few pitches higher without turning into a yell.

Furthermore, the terms *cover* and *covered* might imply a muting or muffling of the sound, qualities not usually desired. For these reasons, most teachers avoid these terms and substitute instead "turning over" and "turned over" as well as "the turn of the voice." In working out the transition zone with a young male, it may be temporarily necessary and useful to overcorrect a strong yell instinct with strategy number one: a deliberate precipitation of the turn, by lowering F1 through moving to a closer vowel and/or slightly longer tube. This maneuver may result in a tone that is too dark, dull, and potentially too heavy for a final product. That would require eventual rebalancing. Subsequently attempting a smooth "timbral glissando" on a single pitch—from an open timbre slowly and smoothly through the turn to a close timbre— may pass through an ideal timbral balance along the way. For example: have a tenor voice sing the following progression: /ɛ e ɪ i/ on a D4, gradually and simultaneously closing the vowel and deepening the timbre. If the larynx is stably low, the timbre should close either on the /e/ or between the /e/ and the /ɪ/, but most definitely by the /i/. A sequence of words containing those vowels may facilitate naturalness of articulation: "bet, bait, bit, beet," or "bed, bayed, bid, bead." Then try this exercise on more or less open versions of the same vowel. If very near its pitch of turning, it should be possible to perform a vowel in open, turning, and close timbres.

Timbral Terminology: Close or Closed

Both adjectives *close* /klos/ and *closed* are found in phonetic literature to describe vowels with a low first formant and convergent resonator shape. There are advantages and disadvantages with either term: *closed* is more properly the opposite of open since *close* means *near* rather than closed. On the other hand, a vowel can be more or less open, but can something be more or less closed? To use an analogy, a door is either open or closed. Once it is open, it *can* be more or less open, but can't be more or less closed. *Closed* does not allow for degrees of a quality. Furthermore, *close* /kloz/ can also be a verb, like open, and as such is useful as a pedagogic directive.

Physically the terms originate from the degree of closeness of the hump of the fronted tongue to the hard palate. A close vowel has the tongue hump close to the hard palate, and an open vowel does not. The tongue can be closer or less close, but it doesn't achieve any physical state that could literally be called closed with vowel articulation, since with vowels there is always some space between the tongue and palate for air and sound to flow out of the mouth.

The International Phonetic Association uses the term *close*. This author has chosen to follow that usage, personally finding it more compatible with the pedagogic concept and use of degrees of closeness (close, more or less closely), opening or closing a vowel further, open and close timbre, etc. Good arguments can be made against *close* for the term *closed*. It is hoped that this semantic difference will neither diminish appreciation of the concept nor prevent its useful practical application.

Register Terminology
This discussion has a long history! Many terms have been employed in the voice science literature of the past fifty years: heavy and light mechanisms, modal and loft, along with chest, head, and falsetto.

Vibrational Modes versus Head and Chest
The most current (though not yet prevalent) designations for vocal registers are:

1) Mode 0 for vocal fry/pulse
2) Mode 1 for thick vocal folds or "chest" (higher contact quotient: greater than ca. 50%)
3) Mode 2 for thin vocal folds or "head" (lower contact quotient: less than ca. 40%)

4) Mode 3 for whistle register

These designations are in reference to the basic **vibrational modes** of the vocal folds across range, rather than primarily to muscles (CT or TA) or to the locations of sensations of vibration (head, chest). They do however arise from particular muscular functions and shapings. Mode one is thought to be TA dominant, and mode two CT dominant. The modes also have attendant acoustic characteristics, and the toggle from mode to mode may be triggered by destabilizing acoustic factors.

This author happily embraces the new terminology, especially for its emphasis on vibrational characteristics. Vibrational mode appears to be binary in almost all singers that have been measured with EGG. That is to say, though excellent singers accomplish smooth *sound* transitions, few singers accomplish an absolutely smooth, gradual shift in vocal fold *shape* and contact quotient. However, thyroarytenoid and cricothyroid muscle involvement across range is not purely binary (on/off). Both are involved to varying extents in many of the vocal fold shapes we use. And there are also shapes for which one or the other is mostly or entirely passive.

There are some who in their zeal for the advantages of this new terminology are rather intolerant of—even indignant toward—use of the old. This is unnecessary. Some continued use of the older terminology has this in its favor: most literature prior to the last decade used it. Unless we refuse to read the historic pedagogic literature, we will at least need to be able to understand and translate these terms. Furthermore, the terms head and chest arose out of real, shared physical vibratory sensations. Human perception of such biofeedback will not disappear with new nomenclature. In that regard, the terms head and chest are general enough in location to allow teachers latitude in specifying sensation location further or not. Finally, it is useful to have terms that can be adapted to indicate degrees of a quality: headier and chestier. (One-ier and two-ier just don't work.)

Some have argued that the old terms indicate a gender bias. On the contrary, we all have heads and chests. Only within pedagogies that strongly associate one or the other with a gender, and limit by gender the use of its complement, is there potential bias. There is no inherent bias in the words themselves, only this possible associative one, which is surely a dying association. Even babies have and use both laryngeal registers. So do well-trained singers.

This author anticipates and welcomes increasing usage of the terminology of vibrational modes. In our acceptance of the new, there is no real need either to erase or avoid historic terminology. It is a fruitless, divisive battle, not worth the trouble, and not likely to be won.

Mix and Falsetto

Another semantic dilemma involves the terms *mix* and *falsetto*. Mix is used in musical theater circles as well as in some Western classical pedagogies to refer to an area of cooperation between TA and CT muscles. It seems perhaps more often to be used to describe a variant of mode one, i.e., to be TA dominant, but with less thickness or vertical phase difference. There are no new muscles involved, and therefore there is no separate mix register *per se*, but it does seem to indicate a subtle but important timbral distinction and a less heavy production. As mentioned earlier, evidence has surfaced recently (Donald Miller, 2013) that attributes this quality to a specific resonance strategy: a clustering of F1 and F2 to resonate the second harmonic between them, in order to continue to keep H2 prominent, even after it has surpassed F1. (H2 prominence is a primary characteristic of belt timbre.)

Falsetto is often understood to be a breathy version of mode two, with a glottal chink between the arytenoids allowing air leakage and a resultant weaker phonation. To others, falsetto is analogous to mode two, something that some have called "reinforced falsetto." If we understand *mix* to be a subcategory of mode one and *falsetto* to be a subcategory of mode two, we should be able to get past semantic differences and continue productive conversation.

Belting and Yelling

This text refers to belting by definition as a skillful form of yelling. This is not intended to be pejorative, nor to suggest that effective belters are just yelling in the manner found for example at sporting events. This is essentially an acoustic observation. The same basic acoustic strategy that is employed in the yell is also employed in belting: a first formant tracking of the second harmonic. However, unskillful yelling is done at abusive pressure levels, often with noise elements that further raise health risks, both of which can result in hoarseness. Well-performed belting is sustainable and does not result in hoarseness or other unhealthy consequences, even with the heavy performance schedules of the musical theater industry. Any high-energy vocalism (operatic singing included)—if done poorly, for too long, within too short of a time span, and without sufficient recovery time—can lead to fatigue, inflammation, and further health issues.

There is however another justification for relating belting to yelling. One of the reasons that belting and its relatives in many forms of world music are so compellingly expressive is precisely their natural connection to yelling. We yell in times of high energy, high emotion, and high stakes. Belting takes full advantage of that natural association. Anyone who teaches healthy belting of course must exercise great care in distinguishing that skill from raw, injurious yelling. Some may prefer to use the term "call" to avoid implying the rough force that can attach to the term "yelling." Nonetheless, from a purely acoustic point of view, the main factor that defines both belt and yell is F1/H2 tracking, hence their associative connection in this text on vocal acoustics. Belting is however a modified, *skillful,* and—when properly done—healthy form of the yell acoustic strategy.

80

Chapter 13
Acoustic Explorations

Exploring Vowel Turning

The following explorations and exercises are good for experiencing the phenomenon and sensations of vowel turning with beginning students as well as for refining its coordination with intermediate and advanced students. Once the basic principles of tube acoustics and harmonic/formant interactions are understood, one's creativity in crafting explorations may be endless. Most of these exercises also assist with exploring the dynamic laryngeal registration needed for free and smooth range negotiation, since the acoustic poles of open timbre and whoop timbre tend respectively to trigger full chest and full head laryngeal register adjustments, and any attempted smooth movement between them provides opportunities for intermediate laryngeal adjustments to occur. (For examples, see Appendix 4 and http://www.kenbozeman.com/)

Beginning Explorations

- On ascending leaps, encourage timbral depth, vowel closeness, and internalized affects and direction (such as sobbiness, mischief, suppressed laugh, or deep conviction). The affective and internalized directional thoughts are meant to counter the "up and out" reaching tendency that typically accompanies the rising larynx of the "yell" instinct.

- Glissando up from an open vowel on a lower pitch over a large interval to a close vowel (and if high enough, into whoop timbre) on a high pitch to identify the poles of kinesthetic and aural sensation. Tube length and laryngeal position should remain constant across the leaps.

- Repeat this on the *same* vowel across its pitch of turning, anticipating, allowing, or if necessary, encouraging its passive modification (by means of the suggestions in the first exploration above).

Figure 33: Open and close vowels and open and close timbre across large leaps.

- Explore turning over in the lower range on the close vowels /i/ and /u/, which turn over well below the location of the *passaggio* as historically understood. This provides sensory experience of the acoustics of turning in an easier context by avoiding the challenges of laryngeal registration posed by the turning locations of the open vowels.

- Speak an inflective loop on each vowel across its pitch of turning, staying deliberately close and deep. Speech inflection across turning is initially much easier than singing across turning. Use affect to motivate the pitch inflection as naturally as possible.

- Sing the following pattern so that the predicted pitch of turning of the vowel is approximately on the 3rd scale degree:

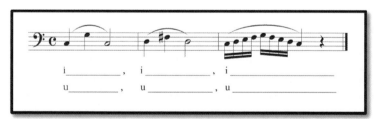

Figure 34: Exploration of turning over, first by leap, then stepwise.

- This can also be done across the F1/H3 crossing of more open vowels an octave and a fifth below their F1 locations, or even the F1/H4 turn two octaves below their F1 locations, allowing

82

- the student to explore timbral shifts and sensations that are parallel to the primary turn, but in an easier part of the range.

Figure 35: Comparing the F1/H2 crossing of /i/ with the F1/H3 crossings of /e/ and the F1/H4 crossing of /ɑ/.

- Sing from a close vowel into a neighboring open vowel and back on the same pitch, and vice versa. Take care to maintain palatal height and remain as convergent as possible on the open vowels.

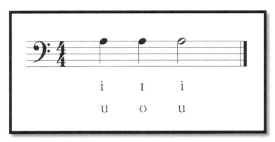

Figure 36: Exploration of close and open timbres. through vowel changes on the same pitch.

It may assist with naturalness to use phrases containing those vowels:

- "He hit me."
- "You would too."

- Other examples (with possible texts) of alternating open and close timbre on the same pitch are listed below. Each example needs to be placed above the turning pitch of the closer vowel, but below the turning pitch of the more open vowel.

/ɪ/→ /i/→/ɪ/   /ʊ/→ /u/→/ʊ/
Tim eats fish.   Would you look?

/i/→ /e/→/i/   /e/→ /i/→/e/
He   ate meat.   They eat late.

/u/→ /o/→/u/   /o/→ /u/→/o/
You know who.   Though you know.

- Explore a repeated pitch across varying degrees of closeness/ openness. Place examples approximately a M6 below the first formant of /i/ for the singer:

/i/→ /ɑ/→/i/: ("We got sleepy.") At this pitch the /i/ will be in close timbre, but the third harmonic of the /ɑ/ will be below F1, making the timbre rather more open.

/i/→ /e/→ /ɑ/→/e/→ /i/: This example will span close to open to more open and back. The use of motivational affect, close articulation, and awareness of F2 placement sensations (Figure 32) will help with timbral unity across these changes.

Intermediate Explorations and Refinement

- This exercise takes the same vowel across two degrees of closure. Place the example so that the primary turn is between the 5th and 8ve. This will go from having H3 below F1 on the first pitch, to H2 below F1 on the second, to turned over/close timbre on the top pitch, and back again.

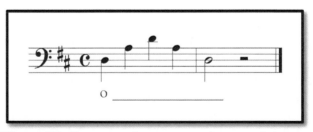

Figure 37: Same vowel across two degrees of closure.

- Sing the following rapid passage, maintaining vowel closeness and depth of timbre. Attempt to shape the dynamics according to the syllable changes, not the pitch changes, with the strongest gesture at the beginning note of each syllable, not at the upward leaps. Independence of intensity and pitch change helps with dynamic laryngeal registration as well as with vowel turning. Rapid passage work discourages changing the vowel shape with pitch changes, promoting facile turning and re-opening:

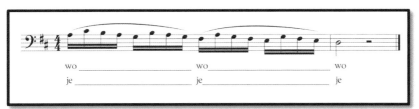

Figure 38: Use of agility across the turn of the voice discourages tube shape change.

- First, model the timbral transition of the F1/H2 crossing during scalar descent, followed immediately by ascent on the same pitches. Descending and opening through the pitch of turning is usually easier and more automatic than ascending and closing. This pattern facilitates immediate and proximate sensory memory of the degree of openness/closeness and passive vowel modification for each pitch of the descent from E4 to B3 as a model for each pitch in the subsequent ascent from B3 to E4:

Figure 39: Modeling the primary acoustic register shift on the descent for the subsequent ascent.

- Ascend and then descend stepwise across the pitch of turning. Initially position the exercise so that the second pitch is the pitch of turning (transitional) and the top pitch fully turned over. This can be done at several pitch levels to include passes that are completely below turning, to those that pass through turning, to those that commence already turned over and in close timbre:

Figure 40: Ascending and then descending stepwise through the primary register shift.

Once the principles and locations of vowel turning are understood, considerable creativity in fashioning exercises or addressing situations in repertoire becomes possible. The primary strategy being used is maintaining tube length while varying the degree of openness/ closeness of the vowels being sung to effect smoother, subtler register transitions with minimal vowel migration and acceptable vowel modification.

Exploring F1/H1 Tracking

The concept of tuning the first formant to the first harmonic (the pitch one is singing) to preserve whoop timbre is simple enough. Once the singer reaches the pitch of the first formant, from there on up the first formant must be raised by vowel opening in tandem with the rising pitch to maintain full resonance and for beneficial feedback on the vibrator. In practice, however, finding the best way to open a vowel is more challenging and nuanced, and requires careful guidance by an expert teacher. As the jaw is lowered further for increased openness of pronunciation, what exactly do the lips and tongue do? Though lip spreading is usually avoided except for extreme high range, is a dead-pan facial expression necessary for freedom or resonance, or may there be some lift in the zygomatic area (pleasantly lifted cheeks)? Does the tongue maintain contact with the upper molars for front vowels, and if so, how high in the range? How much lip rounding can be accommo-dated in the upper voice for the normally lip-rounded vowels? How are these changes from speech shapes best motivated? All of these questions have to do with the issues surrounding active vowel modification and are especially relevant for women and treble voices who frequently sing above the first formant locations of resonant speech vowels.

From an acoustic perspective—combined with some pedagogic opinion of the author—maximizing resonator convergence for the vowel and pitch in question to ensure best resonator feedback and assistance for the vibrator, while extending intelligibility as high as comfortably possible are appropriate goals. In pursuing these goals, the singer should be guided by naturalness and pleasantness of appearance along with comfort and resonance of production. On any given pitch, vowels can retain some visual identity relative to other vowels at that same pitch, regardless of degree of openness. There is no compelling acoustic reason for strangeness of articulation. An unforced call can be used as an approximate shape guide for the appearance of upper voice diction. While the instinctively exaggerated divergence of "called" diction may need modification, some differentiation between vowels is still apparent until quite high. Western classical timbre will need to add a soft palate lift toward the front and some additional openness of throat and settled larynx inside of and below that shape.

A few explorations of the amount of space needed for F1/H1 tracking are offered below for mezzo and soprano voices. Sopranos may find the examples more instructive starting a step higher.

- Sing the following repeated notes, starting on a well formed, "head-dominant" /e/. Glide into the subsequent /i/ with tongue movement only, i.e., without moving the jaw at all. The hump of the tongue should be in contact with the upper molars throughout, but will seem slightly higher on the /i/. This exploration uses the larger vertical opening of the /e/, whose first formant is very near this pitch, to guide the /i/ to a better F1/H1 match. The /i/ may take on some of the quality of an /ɪ/, but ideally should still be convincing as an /i/. The same process should work for /o/ to /u/ and back.

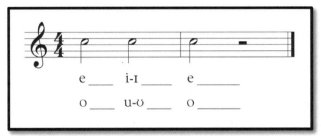

Figure 41. Exploring F1/H1 Tracking #1.

• Next leap from an /i/ a perfect 5th up to an /e/ and back. Repeat, but then insert an /i/ after the /e/ by only changing the tongue, before descending the 5th back to the final /i/. The mouth shape should return to the close position of the initial /i/ on the final /i/. Repeat with /u/ and /o/.

Figure 42. Exploring F1/H1 Tracking #2.

• Next leap up a perfect 5th on an /i/, opening the vowel to match F1 to H1 by dropping the jaw appropriately, but without losing contact between the tongue and the molars, and without dropping the cheeks into a dead pan expression (retain a lightly pleasant expression). Concerning the latter recommendation, a singer's default expression should not be deadpan. In avoiding excessive lateral lip spreading, it is not necessary to remove the subtle lip shaping that comes from light facial expression. In other words, the lip muscles are relaxed and not spread, but "go along for the ride" with the light expressive activation of the cheeks. This strategy also assists in maintaining the sensation of internal height of the tone.

Figure 43. Exploring F1/H1 Tracking #3.

- Finally, begin this exercise with the /zi/ appropriately opened, open further as you ascend, and then close as you descend.

Figure 44. Exploring F1/H1 Tracking #4.

Once the concept and practice of opening a vowel to track H1 is well begun (while retaining other important articulatory aspects: lifted palate, inner smile, open throat, fronted tongue, etc.), most vowel adjustments can be made in any vocalise or in the literature itself. Further attention will be needed to refine the precise manner of opening for each vowel, naturalness of appearance, and to train F1/H1 tracking until it is instinctive.

Chapter 14
Corollary Strategies

This document is focused on practical, applied acoustic pedagogy. Though the principles presented here are vital, acoustic pedagogy will not function well in a pedagogic vacuum, being but one aspect of the whole equation. It is prudent for us to remember not to take part of the truth and make it the whole truth. All of the things that voice teachers routinely do to establish balanced poise of the body, an efficient, responsive breath to voice connection, flow phonation, a freely flowing vibrancy, continuity and suppleness of line, etc., continue to be necessary. Acoustic pedagogy is a valuable partner in this enterprise and can facilitate vocal ease through better interactive coupling of resonation with phonation. A few corollary strategies worth noting in this regard are:

Dynamic Control
Avoid inevitable crescendi with pitch ascent. If an increase in loudness is married to pitch ascent, then probably an increase in pressure is as well, and some resultant movement in the direction of pressed phonation. The student should be able to maintain the same dynamic level during ascending passages. This will be easier when coupled with acoustic pedagogy, since a crescendo on ascent is part of the yell instinct, which is primarily about making very loud sounds. Avoiding opening the vowel and/or raising the larynx at the F1/H2 juncture, and allowing the voice to turn over instead (where appropriate) will enable ascent without crescendo. Also motivating the ascent with some meaningful inflection that does not require a crescendo is a productive corollary strategy (see The Use of Affect below).

Pressure Reduction
A related strategy to counter the tendency to raise breath pressure upon ascent is to use active inhalatory checking of the exhalatory forces of the respiratory system during phonation, specifically by attempting more expansion of the lower chest/middle of the torso to avoid increasing compression of the chest. This is best done with a

feeling of strong yet supple, buoyant, resilient fullness in the breath supply. It is especially helpful to strive for a sense of opening in the chest simultaneous with the perception of a narrowing and collecting of the acoustic sensation of the tone when entering and traversing the *passaggio.*

Vibrancy and Flow

Maintaining vibrancy on all pitches, so that there are no intermittent straight tones in the exercises nor losses of vibrancy at the seams between vowels and/or pitches, also helps avoid pressed phonation and the pressure increase that accompanies it. Movement, either of the entire body or with arm gesture to model the flow and shape of the phrase is a familiar strategy to avoid holding or locking up in the respiratory/phonatory connection/coordination.

The Use of Affect

Voice is motivated by expression. This is apparently inherent and primal. The first thing a newborn does is to inhale. The very next thing most newborns do is to phonate, communicating quite expressively how they feel about what just happened. Very few spontaneous phonations in life are not caused by the impulse to communicate (exceptions include sounds accompanying sneezing, coughing, throat clearing, hiccups). Not only emotional quality, but also tessitura and pitch change are motivated by expressive inflection. We change pitch inflection without planning, merely by the expressive intent that is motivating our speaking. In music, melodic notation is really a kind of choreography for expressive inflection. The task of the singer is to intuit the expressive motivation that would automatically result in the given melodic contour.

Affect can be very useful in inspiring inflective loops across the pitch of turning. In general, deepening, internalizing affects are most useful for ascending inflections as well as for upward melodic leaps. For example, speak the phrase, "Oh, I get it," with an inflective loop up and back down on the "oh," knowingly expressing the deep realization of an epiphany. Do this while thinking a close /o/ and an internalized (in, down and out) direction into the body, as if "drinking the tone." This can help to promote good acoustic and laryngeal registration— i.e., sufficiently suppress the yell instinct—during the excursion.

Affects that encourage greater CT involvement (i.e., a lighter, "headier" laryngeal registration) as well as a favorable convergent poise of the resonator also can assist upper range excursions. Examples of such affects are sweetness, love, reassurance, compassion, sobbiness, self-pity, mischief, and self-satisfaction, most of which are in some sense internalizing affects. Examples of affects that tend to increase TA involvement are authority, confidence, anger, hatred, machismo, and projected egotism, that is, affects that are more externally focused. For a robust, yet lyric laryngeal registration, joy and enthusiasm are motivationally helpful.

The Problem of Micromanagement

Like most physical coordinations, singing is not an activity that responds well to micromanagement. Timbral transitions that should occur purely as the result of pitch change—and the resultant changing relationships between harmonics and the first formant—ideally should not be manipulated or micromanaged. They should feel to the singer more like acoustic than like muscular events. While specific awareness and attention to turning over may initially be needed to overcome the yell instinct and habit, the more generalized and holistic the eventual motivation, and the subtler the effects of turning, the better. It is often preferable to stimulate appropriate vowel turning indirectly as a by-product of a different directive or motivation, such as diction, affect, or a directional gesture. Furthermore, once a voice becomes accustomed through repetition and habituation to allowing vowels to close at their predicted locations, turning over need neither be volitional nor self-conscious.

Chapter 15
Laryngeal Registration Revisited

This text is deliberately focused on voice acoustics, with minimal reference to other crucial biomechanical aspects of voice pedagogy (anatomy, breathing, etc.), all of which are important in their own right and interact significantly with the acoustics of production. However laryngeal registration is so directly involved in and interactive with voice source acoustics, it will receive some brief attention here.

From an acoustic point of view, what is needed from the voice source is a clean, clear, relatively consistent, usually strong set of harmonics appropriate to the range and dynamic level required of the situation. The singer must also be capable of traversing the range without perceivably abrupt changes in the source input, even when crossing from one vibrational mode to another, such as from "chest" to "head." Acoustic interaction and feedback are often involved in smoothing these transitions, but we should first consider the necessary muscular adjustments themselves.

Muscle Action

A prominent theory postulates that the two primary, mutually antagonistic muscular functions of the larynx that shape the vocal folds—the shortening, thickening TA's and the lengthening, thinning CT's—cooperate in an overlapping middle range to achieve a smooth "baton exchange" by very gradually shifting the proportions of their involvement. Though perceptually smooth register transitions are heard in performances of excellent singers, a perfectly smooth transfer of muscle activity, in which one group tapered involvement gradually down to zero, has rarely been measured. There is almost always a point at which a binary toggle from greater vocal fold contact to thinner vocal fold contact occurs, even when accomplished essentially inaudibly. There is probably an aerodynamic or acoustic factor at play that triggers this observable change. Nevertheless, it is a very fruitful strategy to practice absolute perceptual smoothness of laryngeal registration across range.

Downstream Resisters and Semi-Occluded Vocal Tracts

One effective approach is to glissando across the entire range using some helpful **downstream resister** or **semi-occluded vocal tract** articulation. A downstream resister is any articulator position or function that requires or resists airflow and is downstream from the vocal folds, i.e., nearer to or at the lips. If the resister is a vibrator, like a tongue or lip trill, it will require steady airflow and pressure to be vibrated. The vocal folds must allow enough flow through to drive the downstream resister. If it is a semi-occluded articulation at or near the lips, it increases inertive reactance, lowering the phonation threshold pressure (the amount of pressure needed to bring the vocal folds into vibration). Either strategy reduces pressed phonation. Downstream resisters or semi-occluded articulations that can be used in glissandi for smoothing laryngeal register shifts include:

1) Tongue trills
2) Lip trills/raspberries/blubbering
3) Phonating through a short straw
4) A buzzy hum or buzzing through a lightly bite-held lower lip (modified /v/).
5) "Kazooing" through a tiny /w/ or fricative /β/.
6) Open mouthed /ŋ/ or other nasal consonants such as /n m/

Motivating Laryngeal Stability

With any of these glissandi, care should be taken not to allow the larynx to rise when approaching the primary register transition (ca. B3-G4). This can be helped by motivating the phonation in that transitional range with expressive inflection or with affects that stabilize the throat shape and laryngeal depth, such as:

1) Self-pitying whimper
2) "Up to no good but pleased with yourself" mischief
3) Suppressed laughter
4) Sobbiness

These affects can apparently be done rather strongly without risk of injury or even of muscle rigidity. As with yawning, these affective actions are self-limiting, with muscles working in antagonism with inherent tissue elasticity. Though the student may be inclined instinctively to relax affective positioning when opening for upper range, resonance and vocal tract structural poise are better served by strengthening the affect with ascent.

Laryngeal Registration Goals

The goals of laryngeal registration are a clean, clear, light, voice source "buzz" throughout the entire compass with no pressure surges, minimal pressure increase, and with a stable larynx and throat space. Maintaining throat space when ascending through the *zona di passaggio* may need to be more deliberate. Since these exercises are not executed on open-mouthed vowels, they moderate some of the acoustic effects that might otherwise destabilize register transitions. This allows the focus of attention to be exclusively on the smoothness and ease of the voice source laryngeal "buzz" across range.

Glissando-ing on a vowel poses more challenges, but would be the next step after downstream resisters. It is usually easier to glissando on naturally convergent vowels, such as /i/, provided the vowel is opened gradually and sufficiently to formant track H1 when approaching whoop timbre and above.

Chapter 16
Instructional Technology

As mentioned in the introduction, instructional technology is now readily available, inexpensive, and rather user-friendly. Each application or program does take some training to understand its most appropriate uses. Other texts have written more extensively on this, but this chapter will give a summary of two instruments and their use.

The *Madde* Voice Synthesizer

Throughout this text explorations using the *Madde* /mɑd:ə/ voice synthesizer have been recommended to illustrate both aurally and visually various aspects of vocal acoustics. This author considers *Madde* to be a most helpful tool for vocal acoustics explanations. It is a free shareware product from Swedish engineer Svante Granqvist, which is programmable to represent any voice type on any vowel singing any pitch within a standard keyboard. *Madde* clearly displays

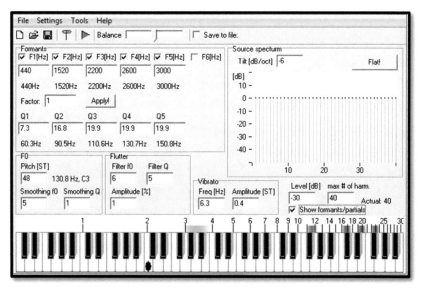

Figure 45: *Madde* voice synthesizer, displaying voice source harmonics (numbered lines) and formants (red bands) just above the keyboard.

both harmonics (with numbered lines) and formants (with red shaded bands) above a keyboard, an especially musician-friendly feature. This format provides the simplest, most direct way to explain to students the effects of harmonic/formant interactions so crucial to acoustic vocal registration. *Madde* can be useful for occasional explanations in the studio, and even for audio demonstrations of harmonic/formant interactions and the passive vowel modifications that accompany them, but it is especially well suited for voice pedagogy classes. *Madde* can be used to illustrate 1) the effect of pitch on the number of harmonics within useful range, 2) the roll-off (tilt) in power of the source harmonics, 3) the effect of the presence or absence of formants, and 4) the aural effects of all harmonic/formant interactions.

Limitations of *Madde*

Madde and Modes of Phonation

Madde can roughly model different vibrational modes (head or chest) by varying the tilt or "roll off" of the voice source (see Appendix 1: *Madde* Exploration 2) and, to some extent, modes of phonation (pressed, breathy, flow). However since the voice source input of harmonics in *Madde* is always "clean" or noise-free, it cannot accurately model breathy phonation, which typically has an air-noise element. Since no muscles are involved in its voice source, neither can it really model all of the timbral changes that accompany pressed phonation.

Madde and Non-Linearity

Madde is strictly **linear** (non-interactive) and therefore cannot model the effects of non-linearity on the voice source or on resonation. In other words, the resonances/formants one programs do not cause changes in the source input—as can happen in a human voice—but merely selectively resonate its harmonics.

Madde and Vibrato

Since *Madde's* programmed vibrato cycles—though adjustable in rate and extent—are essentially uniform, audible pitch undulations are more apparent and distracting than in a real voice with an ideal vibrato. With actual voices, minute waveform variability can help to create a perceptual "singleness of pitch," if rate and extent parameters are within certain limits. That is to say, a tone can be consistently vibrant (have measureable regular *frequency* undulations) without any perceivable *pitch* undulation. Bear in mind that pitch is not the same as frequency. It is the term for our *perception* of frequency. In a real voice, if the vibrato frequency is close to six per second and the extent (excursion above and below the target frequency) is a semi-tone, while we perceive that something is moving, the pitch sounds stable rather than wobbly or tremulous. One student described his perception upon hearing an ideal vibrato as "movement within the pitch rather than movement of the pitch." This is analogous to our perceiving a smoothly moving picture when in fact twenty-four still frames per second are flashed on the screen at the theater. Perceptual and actual phenomena diverge. *Madde* does not replicate this "singleness of pitch" phenomenon.

In spite of these few limitations, because of its musician friendly keyboard display and general excellence of design, Svante Granqvist's *Madde* voice synthesizer is an outstanding instructional tool—the best available to date—for acoustics presentations/explanations for under-graduate voice pedagogy classes or for any audience. It is strongly recommended that you download and use *Madde* for the explorations described in this text for best understanding of the principles and sounds being discussed.

Madde can be downloaded to PCs or Macs that can handle Windows applications from the following site:

http://www.tolvan.com

Spectrography
The instructional technology that is the simplest to read and the most useful for the voice studio is **real time spectrography**. *Real time* means that the analysis is simultaneous and the image display immediate—essentially as the sound is happening, i.e., in real time. Spectrography is an analysis of sound that isolates the frequency com-ponents of the sound and displays them on the vertical dimension, with higher frequencies lying higher across the graph, and lower frequencies lying lower. Time moves horizontally across the graph, with the present instant entering on the right edge of the screen and

then scrolling to the left. Saved images are then read from left (earliest sound) to right (most recent sound). A third dimension—the intensity or power of the frequency components—is displayed on a color or darkness scale. Of all the ways we analyze and graph sound, the spectrographic image is visually the most analogous to sound over time, and therefore the most approachable, understandable, and even intuitive for students. With minimal initial explanation, students can both see and hear important characteristics of their singing in the playback, leading to productive commentary or discussion. This author has experimented with real time spectrography since 1989 and had the privilege of using spectrography in his voice studio since 1993. It is as ever present as the mirror on the wall and is referred to at a comparable rate—that is, only as needed and when helpful.

VoceVista

Real time spectrography is readily available from various sources in various forms, including the deservedly popular **VoceVista** program, developed by Donald Miller, Harm Schutte, and their research team in Groningen, Netherlands. (See figure 46). If the program's analysis parameters are set to display a **narrow frequency bandwidth** (see definitions), which is the default setting for *Voce Vista*, the individual **harmonics** of the voice can easily be seen flowing horizontally across the screen, and therefore characteristics of vibrato and vocal line can be monitored and evaluated. While **broad bandwidth** settings show vocal tract **formants** even more clearly, formants are usually reason-ably apparent with the narrow width default settings, especially for low and mid-range pitches, such that overall resonance and **resonance balance** can also be monitored with them. Durational parameters can be set to save short segments of time for near immediate retrieval, listening, and viewing. Continuity and consistency of vibrancy, brevity of consonantal interruption, and consistency of resonance balance, among other things, can be readily seen and heard on playback.

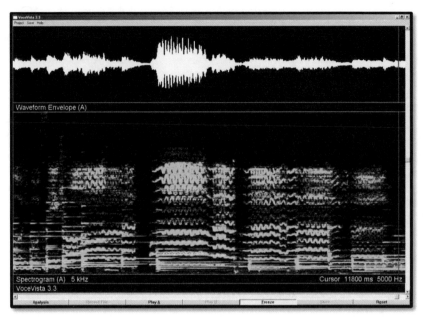

Figure 46: *VoceVista* real time spectrography, with frequency on the vertical, time on the horizontal, intensity on the color scale, with the pressure waveform displayed above.

Power Spectra

If more detailed display or research is needed, a **power spectrum** display, and even **electroglottography** (EGG) can be used (both available with *VoceVista*). Power spectra display power or intensity on the vertical and frequency (spectrum) on the horizontal. Unlike spectrography, which graphs segments of time on the horizontal, power spectra usually only graph an instant (either the present instant or an instant selected from a saved spectrograph) of time. Power spectra can therefore show formants, harmonics, and their relative strengths in great detail (see figure 47).

Electroglottography (EGG)

Electroglottography is a charting of the amount of glottal contact in each vibratory cycle, from which a closed quotient (percentage of time the glottis is closed) and laryngeal register can be postulated. Data is collected by means of a small electric current passing between two electrodes placed one on either side of the larynx. The greater the conductivity between them, the greater the vocal fold contact. Chest voice has greater vocal fold contact and a larger contact quotient than head voice. Therefore one can—roughly at least—estimate vibrational mode from contact quotient.

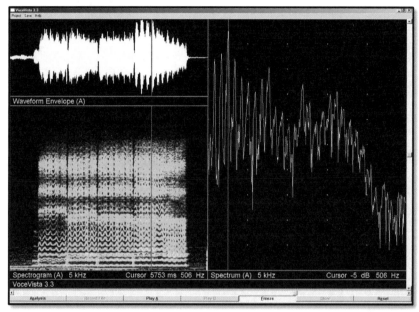

Figure 47. *VoceVista* with waveform (top left), spectrograph (bottom left), and power spectrum (right) displayed. The vertical time cursor on the left selects the moment being displayed on the power spectrum. The short horizontal frequency cursor on the spectrograph (the third harmonic from the bottom) becomes the vertical cursor on the power spectrum.

Though EGG signals can give very specific information about **laryngeal registration** and its coordination with acoustic factors, both essential in ongoing research, it is not yet clear that what electroglottography adds is sufficiently crucial to be necessary for regular weekly lesson use. For more information on EGG (as well as for any matters of vocal resonance), this author highly recommends Donald Miller's *Resonance in Singing*. (See Selected References). Suggested uses of *VoceVista* in the studio will be addressed below.

Studio Uses of *Voce Vista*

VoceVista is a powerful, well-designed tool for voice analysis and research. As argued earlier, real-time spectrography—which is available from various sources including *VoceVista*—is the most intuitively analogous way to graph sound visually. With frequency on the vertical, time on the horizontal, and intensity on the color or brightness scale, its display is understandable and readable by students after minimal training. Very practical matters of vocal line are readily apparent: continuousness and consistency of vibrancy, dynamic shaping, duration of any interruption of the tonal flow, and at least in a general sense, timbral balance. This author therefore has real-time spectrography running essentially continuously in lessons as the standard technology for playback. If a more detailed look at the relative strength of harmonics is needed, a screen display that includes power spectrum can be selected. Power spectrum typically displays one instant of time, with power (intensity) on the vertical and frequency (spectrum) on the horizontal. *VoceVista* very handily coordinates the spectrograph display with the power spectrum display so that one can scroll through the time dimension of the spectrograph and examine each instant in detail on the power spectrum.

Spectrographic display is best for assessing:
1) Vibrancy (immediacy, consistency, continuity)
2) Vocal line (tonal and general timbral continuity)
3) General sense of overall resonance
4) General presence and strength of the singer's formant cluster

Things that spectrography is not best suited for include:
1) Close comparisons between fairly similar vowels (Power spectra are better.)
2) Subtle timbral distinctions
3) Determining which sounds are correct (Your trained ear decides. The picture may or may not show evidence, depending upon the nature and degree of difference.)
4) Best laryngeal height (Your ear, eye, and the student's freedom of function are better.)

5) Precise formant/harmonic interactions (Power spectra and your ear are better.)

That said, the audio playback of *VoceVista* that accompanies the visual display is good enough to "complete the picture" of most issues being discussed. Ultimately, it is the sound—and accompanying freedom of sensation—that determine the success of the singing being evaluated. Spectrography doesn't tell you what is good, bad, or indifferent. It simply displays what is. The teacher and student look, listen and discuss to determine what the sounds and the graph are reflecting.

Definitions

Acoustic Registration: the timbral transitions that occur as a result of harmonic/formant interactions. All acoustic register events involve harmonic interactions with the first formant. Many also involve interaction with the second formant.

Articulation: in speech and singing, the shaping or tuning of the vocal tract to modify the filtered voice source signal; articulation also includes how the tongue, lips, jaw, and other speech organs are involved in the production of consonant sounds.

Aryepiglottic sphincter: the mouth of the epilarynx, formed by the tissues connecting the epiglottis with the arytenoids. A narrowing of the aryepiglottic sphincter is associated with a boost in upper partials from the voice source. It is part of the resonance strategy of singer's formant cluster in Western classical singing and of the ring or twang of belt production.

Bandwidths: a tube resonance has a certain frequency range contour; that is, it will reinforce frequencies to either side of its peak frequency, covering a range of frequencies. If the contour of the resonance is a tall, narrow peak, it has a narrow bandwidth. If its contour is more of a bell curve shape, it has a wider bandwidth. Brass instrument resonances have very narrow bandwidths, and will therefore only pass specific harmonics of a given tube length through. Vocal tract resonances (formants) have wider bandwidths, allowing more voice source harmonics through on either side of the peak formant frequency.

Belting: a singing style with a mode one-dominant laryngeal registration, using an acoustic strategy in which the first formant tracks the second harmonic; in other words, a kind of skillful yelling. Some form of belt is prevalent in many forms of popular, folk, and world music and in American musical theater.

Breathy phonation: (see Mode of phonation)

Chesty: (see Laryngeal register)

Chiaroscuro: an Italian term meaning "bright-dark" borrowed from art history to describe an ideal resonance balance between low and high frequency components in Western classical singing. It is usually accomplished (in middle and lower ranges) by some balance in power between the first formant and the singer's formant cluster.

Closed Quotient: the average percentage of time the glottis is closed during one vibratory cycle. A large closed quotient would usually indicate a chestier laryngeal register with a short, thick vocal fold shape (vibrational mode one). A smaller closed quotient would usually indicate a headier laryngeal register with a long, thin vocal fold shape (vibrational mode two). (See Contact quotient)

Close timbre: a vocal sound in which the second harmonic has risen above the first formant, causing the voice to "turn over." Also termed _voce chiusa_ in Italian.

Close vowel: a vowel with a low first formant such as /i/ and /u/ and an inherently convergent resonator shape.

Contact Quotient: the degree of vocal fold contact in a given vibratory cycle. A large contact quotient would usually indicate a chestier laryngeal register with a short, thick shape (vibrational mode one). A smaller contact quotient would usually indicate a headier laryngeal register with a long, thin shape (vibrational mode two). Though related to closed quotient, it is possible to have a high contact quotient without complete glottal closure, or a high closed quotient (duration of closure) without deep contact, but it is more typical to have a high closed quotient when there is a high contact quotient. EGG displays contact quotient reliably, from which closed quotient may be less reliably inferred.

Convergent resonator: a vocal tract shape that is relatively (for the vowel being produced) more open near the glottis and narrower near the lips (the inverted megaphone). Such a resonance strategy is typical of Western classical singing and _voce chiusa_.

Cover: the timbral shift that accompanies the F1/H2 crossing; turning over.

Cricothyroid muscles (CT): (see Laryngeal register)

Depth: a description of the timbre of a sound that has significant strength in one of its lowest harmonics, as resonated by the first formant.

Divergent resonator: a description of a resonator shape that is smaller in the pharynx and more open nearer the lips. Open vowels are inherently divergent in shape. This resonance strategy is typical of musical theater as well as many world music singing styles.

Downstream resister: any resister (articulator position or device that resists airflow to some extent) that is downstream from the vocal folds, i.e., nearer to or at the lips. Downstream resisters share the pressure load from the lungs with the vocal folds, necessitating higher airflow through the glottis and reducing the pressure difference across the vocal folds. This inhibits pressing. (See also Semi-occluded vocal tract)

Electroglottography (EGG): a charting of the amount of glottal contact in each vibratory cycle, from which a closed quotient (the percentage of time the glottis is closed) and laryngeal register can be postulated. Data is collected by means of a small electric current passing between two electrodes placed one on either side of the larynx. The greater the conductivity between them, the greater the vocal fold contact. Chest voice (mode one) has greater vocal fold contact and a larger contact quotient than head voice (mode two).

Epilarynx: the short tube formed by the epiglottis and the aryepiglottic folds and arytenoids just above the vocal folds. The epilarynx forms a small tube within the larger tube of the laryngopharynx. Narrowing of the aryepiglottic sphincter (the exit of the epilarynx) increases acoustic reactance and boosts higher frequencies.

Fach: a German term for specific voice categories, such as soubrette soprano, Heldentenor, Verdi baritone, etc., which are determined by the tessitura capacity, vocal "weight," and timbre of a voice. The overall location of vocal tract formants, as well as the specific location of the singer's formant cluster are significant factors in determining quality and therefore the *Fach* of a singer.

Flow phonation: (see Mode of phonation)

Formant: a natural resonance of the vocal tract, caused by standing waves in the quarter wave resonator.

> **Vowel formants:** the first (lowest) two formants of the vocal tract are also the most tunable, and therefore the most significant in defining the vowel quality of a sound. Together they are called the vowel formants.

> **Singer's formant cluster:** a clustering of formants three and above (usually formants 3-5) generated by a low larynx, open laryngopharynx, and narrowed epilaryngeal tube exit, that results in an increase in power in the high frequency components of a sung sound. It is especially characteristic of males in Western classical singing, enabling them to carry over orchestral accompaniment.

Formant detuning: the tuning of a formant frequency peak away from a harmonic to weaken its effect. Used with F2 in female/treble upper range to reduce shrillness and with F1 in males voices to avoid whoop timbre on close vowels.

Formant tracking: the tuning of a formant to follow or track a specific harmonic, such as F1/H1 tracking of whoop timbre (upper female voice strategy) or F1/H2 tracking of the yell or of belting.

Formant tuning: the tuning of one or both of the first two formants in order to find a better formant/harmonic match for greater resonance.

Front-back dimension: a description either of a physical articulatory characteristic (a fronted tongue hump verses a tongue hump further back), or of an acoustic characteristic (a sound with a high second formant and therefore stronger high partials, i.e., a front vowel; or a low second formant and therefore weaker high partials and potentially stronger low partials, i.e., a back vowel).

Fullness: a typical descriptor of a sound with significant strength in its lowest harmonics, as resonated by the first formant. Other similar terms are: depth, warmth, roundness.

Fundamental frequency (F_o): the lowest harmonic of a sound (H1), more or less equivalent to the perceived pitch.

Harmonic: a frequency component of a sound. Harmonic frequency components are either the lowest component (the fundamental frequency) or whole integer multiples of the lowest frequency component. Together they therefore generate a pressure waveform that repeats at the frequency of that lowest common denominator.

Heavy Cover: deliberate lowering of F1 (by tube lengthening and vowel closing) to precipitate the turning over of the voice. Strategies used include lowering the larynx, lip rounding and/or trumpeting, and vowel darkening.

Helmholtz Resonator: a hollow enclosure having a small opening consisting of such dimensions that the enclosure resonates at a single frequency determined by the dimensions of the space and the opening.

Inertive reactance: a sluggishness of air molecule movement created by resonator convergence, which can improve resonator interactivity with the vibrator.

Laryngeal register: the muscular adjustment of the vocal folds; the relative participation of the thryoarytenoid (TA—shortening, thickening) muscles and the cricothyroid (CT—stretching, thinning) muscles.

> **Chesty:** historic description of a sound assumed to be TA dominant, with shorter, thicker, looser vocal folds, and which has more strong high harmonic component frequencies. Now called vibrational **mode one**.

> **Cricothyroid muscles (CT):** the muscles, which upon contracting stretch and thin the vocal folds for higher pitches. They are mostly situated outside of the larynx and tilt the laryngeal cartilages to stretch the vocal folds. They are

responsible for what has historically been called "head" or "falsetto" register (now vibrational **mode two**), with its thinner vocal fold contact, fundamental frequency dominance, and smaller number of harmonics.

Heady: historic description of a sound assumed to be CT dominant, with thinner, longer, tauter vocal folds, and which has a stronger fundamental and fewer and weaker high harmonic component frequencies. Now called vibrational **mode two**.

Thyroarytenoid muscles (TA): the muscles, which upon contracting shorten and thicken the vocal folds for lower pitches. They comprise the body of the vocal folds and are responsible for what has historically been called "chest" register (now vibrational **mode one**), with its thicker vocal fold contact, **vertical phase difference**, and larger number of harmonics.

Linear source-filter model: a model of vocal resonance that is spacially linear, that is, that postulates a power source (breath) providing airflow to a vibrator (vocal folds), bringing them into vibration, generating a voice source signal (sound wave) containing harmonics, which are then selectively resonated by a filter (resonator; vocal tract), which transfers the filtered harmonics to the outside world through the lips.

Mode of phonation: a way of categorizing the ratios of the three elements of a phonation: breath pressure (above atmospheric, generated below the glottis), airflow (through the glottis), and glottal resistance (vocal valve closure force). Although these can vary along a continuum, they can be modeled by representative numbers in a **phonation equation** as follows: breath pressure/airflow = glottal resistance. One of three ratios of pressure, flow, and glottal resistance of a phonation: breathy (excess airflow: $1/2 = .5$); pressed (excess glottal resistance or glottal closure force: $1/.5 = 2$); flow (a balance between pressure, flow, and resistance: $1/1 = 1$). (Not to be confused with vibrational mode—see Laryngeal registration above.)

> **Breathy phonation:** a phonation equation model with excess airflow, such as $1/\underline{2} = .5$ would be termed breathy phonation.

> **Flow phonation:** a phonation equation model with an ideal balance for a given situation would be $1/1=1$, and is termed flow phonation.

> **Pressed phonation:** a phonation equation model with excess glottal resistance, such as $1/.5 = \underline{2}$ would be termed pressed phonation.

Mode one: a vibrational mode of the voice source in which the vocal fold shape is short and thick, and the vocal fold cover loose. It has **vertical phase difference**, generating more and stronger high partials. It is caused by greater TA laryngeal muscle participation. (See Laryngeal register)

Mode three: a vibrational mode of the voice source in which the vocal fold shape is long and thin, and the vocal fold cover is taut. However, the vocal folds may not be fully adducted nor vibrate along their full length.

Mode two: a vibrational mode of the voice source in which the vocal fold shape is long and thin, and the vocal fold cover is taut. It has little **vertical phase difference**, resulting in a more sinusoidal pressure wave that is more fundamental frequency dominant. It is caused by greater CT laryngeal muscle participation and usually passive TAs. (See Laryngeal register)

Mode zero: a vibrational mode of the voice source in which the vocal fold shape is short and thick, and the vocalis muscle and vocal fold cover are loose. Also called pulse or vocal fry register.

Non-linear source-filter model: a source-filter model of vocal resonance with the added component of possible interactivity between the filter and the source, such that certain resonation postures of the filter cause feedback on the vibrator that alters the function and contribution of the vibrator, ideally by assisting its efficiency.

Openness-closeness dimension: descriptions of a vocal sound relative to the frequency location of its first formant and to the relationship of its harmonics to its first formant. (See *Voce chiusa,* Close timbre, Close vowel, and *Voce aperta,* Open timbre, Open vowel)

Open timbre: a vocal sound in which two or more harmonics are at or below the first formant of the vowel being sung. Also termed *voce aperta* in Italian. Sometimes also used to describe a generally divergent resonance shape strategy.

Open vowel: a vowel with a high first formant, such as /ɑ/, and an inherently divergent resonator shape.

Overtones: a designation for frequency components of a sound that lie above the fundamental frequency. Overtones usually refer to harmonic frequencies. The first overtone is the second harmonic.

Partials: another term for frequency components of a sound; partials may also refer to non-harmonic frequencies, i.e., frequencies that are not multiples of the lowest frequency component.

Passaggio: Italian for passage or transition into the upper voice.

> *Primo passaggio:* the lower entry into the transition zone.

> *Secondo passaggio:* the upper exit of the transition zone, entry into the upper voice.

> *Zona di passaggio:* the transition zone, a range segment of about a 4th or 5th in males, during which it is thought that the laryngeal registration should shift from a TA dominant mode one to a lighter mode one with greater CT participation. In female registration this transition area is longer and is sub-divided into a lower middle and upper middle, during which the voice transitions into CT dominant vibrational mode two.

Passive vowel modification: this author's proposed designation for a change in vowel quality accomplished by retaining the vocal tract

PRACTICAL VOCAL ACOUSTICS

shape but moving the pitch with its set of harmonics. The change in vowel quality results from the changing relationships and interactions between the stable formants and the moving harmonics. (See Vowel modification.)

Piriform Sinuses (Fossae):   the small side branches of the lower pharynx to either side of the laryngopharynx which create an anti-resonance in the 4000-6000Hz region, highlighting the singer's formant cluster just below.

Pitch: our perception of the frequency of a sound. It is the frequency of the composite pressure pattern of the multiple frequencies of a tone.   In most practical circumstances, it can be considered the equivalent of the fundamental frequency.

Pitch of turning: the pitch at which a voice turns over, just inside of an octave below the pitch of the first formant of the vowel being sung. The pitch at which the H2 crosses above the F1 of the vowel being sung.

Power spectrum: a power spectrum is an analysis of a sound that displays power on the vertical and frequency components on the horizontal.

Pressed phonation: (see Mode of phonation)

Pressure waveform: the pattern of air pressure variations that form a sound. If there is a regular pattern that repeats periodically, the sound will have a clear pitch. If there is no regularly repeating pattern, rather a random pressure variation, the sound will be perceived as noise.

Primary acoustic register transitions: prominent acoustic registration events at the point at which H2 crosses F1, transitioning from open to close timbre, and the point at which H1 intersects F1, attaining whoop timbre.   Refining these two events is a major goal of Western classical singing pedagogy for men and women, respectively. The former is most often associated with the turning over of the open vowels in the neighborhood of C4-G4 in male voices. The latter is the preferred strategy for the upper range of Western classical female singing.

112

Primary laryngeal register transition: the shift from chest to falsetto, or vibrational mode one to vibrational mode two. Male classical singers tend to avoid this shift, staying in some form of mode one for the entire range. Female classical singers tend to shift from mode one to mode two between C4 and G4, usually before (below) the F1/H2 acoustic register transition. Belters extend mode one or chest register to ca. C5.

Quarter-wave resonator: a resonator that is a tube open at one end and closed at the other. Such a resonator can establish standing waves (resonances) at the quarter-wave length, and odd numbered multiples of that length: 3/4 wave length, 5/4 wave length, 7/4 wave length, etc. The vocal tract is a form of quarter wave resonator, but with more variable, tunable wavelengths.

Reactance: a matching of resistance between the glottis and the vocal tract or epilarynx that increases the interactivity of the system (feed-back on the vibrator).

Resonance: Resonance is the tendency of an object or system to respond (oscillate) more strongly to particular frequencies introduced into it.

Real time spectrography: an ever-changing, immediately current analysis and visual representation of sound that displays frequency on the vertical, time on the horizontal, and intensity on the grey or color scale. This form of sound display is perhaps the most intuitive and informative as a visual learning aide for students.

Roll off: the drop in intensity of harmonics above the first harmonic; typically indicated in decibels per octave (dBs/octave). Called "Tilt" on the *Madde* synthesizer.

Semi-occluded vocal tract: a vocal tract with an exit sufficiently narrowed to generate flow resistance or acoustic impedance. A short thin straw is one mechanical example. A very small, kazoo-like /w/ is an articulatory example. (See also Downstream resister.)

Singer's formant cluster: (see Formant)

Spectral envelope: an outline of the power dimension of a power spectrum. It is useful for revealing the resonance characteristics (formants) of a particular vocal tract shape.

Spectrography: a spectrograph displays frequency on the vertical, time on the horizontal, and power on the grey or color scale. It is perhaps the most accessible display of sound for studio use.

Thyroarytenoid muscles (TA): (see Laryngeal register)

Turning over: the passing of H2 above F1 of a voice, and its accompanying sound and sensation.

Valsalva maneuver: a forceful compression of the thorax (ribcage); similar to effortful elimination, childbearing, heavy lifting. If resisted by glottal closure, it stimulates excessively strong glottal resistance and should not be used in singing.

Vertical phase difference: a difference in the timing of opening and closing of the vocal folds' vertical contact. It is caused by a thicker vocal fold whose contact area opens and closes at its lower margins ahead of the opening and closing of its upper margins.

Vocal tract filter: the tube resonator comprised of the vocal tract from the glottis to the lips. This resonator "filters" the harmonics passed through it, strengthening some and weakening others to create the vowels and timbre of the sound radiated from the lips.

Voce aperta: open timbre; any sung sounds in which two or more harmonics are at or below the first formant—in other words, the timbre of any pitches sung an octave or more below the first formant. This term has also been used historically to describe an overall divergent resonator shape characterized by open timbre, in which vowels tend to spread and move into yell timbre, and more typical of belting and various world music singing styles.

Voce chiusa: close timbre; any sung sounds in which the second harmonic is above the first formant—in other words, the timbre of any pitches within an octave below the first formant. This term has also been used historically to describe an overall convergent resonator poise that results in the *chiaroscuro* timbre of Western classical singing, in

114

which vowels close when and where they should, in contrast to a predominantly divergent, open timbre resonator adjustment.

Voice source: the sound signal produced at the vibrator (vocal folds).

Vowel formants: (see Formant)

Vowel modification: historically understood to refer to a change in the vowel quality accomplished by moving the vowel formants from their normal speech locations by means of changes in the shape of the vocal tract in an attempt to find better (more resonant) formant/harmonic matches. This text proposes the subcategories: active and passive vowel modification. (See Passive vowel modification)

Yell coupling, yell timbre: an acoustic coupling of F1 and H2 that has been carried higher than normal through tube shortening and mouth widening (F1/H2 tracking); bright and often pressed and spread in quality.

Abbreviations

A4, B3, C5, etc.: pitch designations by octave with A4 corresponding to 440 Hz, and C4 corresponding to middle C.

CT: Cricothyroid muscle

F_o: the fundamental frequency or lowest frequency component of a sound (the same as H1).

F1, F2, F3, etc.: formants of the vocal tract filter function. The vocal tract is a resonator with multiple natural resonances, called formants that are numbered from lowest to highest.

H1, H2, H3, etc.: harmonics from the voice source: the frequency components of a tuned sound that has "pitch."

IPA: international phonetic alphabet. IPA symbols for vowels appear in the following form in this text: /ɑ/.

M0, M1, M2, M3: vibrational modes of the vocal folds, corresponding roughly to the historic terms pulse, chest, head, and whistle.

SFC: Singer's formant cluster, a clustering of formants three and higher.

TA: Thyroarytenoid muscle

116

Appendix 1: *Madde* Explorations

Madde Exploration 1: the unresonated voice source.

Check the "Show formants/partials" box (bottom right just above the keyboard). Uncheck the formants boxes (upper left, labeled F1[Hz], F2[Hz], F3[Hz], etc.). Activate a set of harmonics by clicking on a pitch on the keyboard at or below middle C (middle C4 is marked with a black dot). You will see a set of numbered lines, representing the harmonics of the pitch you selected, just above the keyboard. (See Figure 1.) Activate the play arrow (top left). This will approximate the pitched buzz of an un-resonated set of harmonics as it might sound immediately above the glottis. You will probably want to deactivate this unattractive sound fairly quickly.

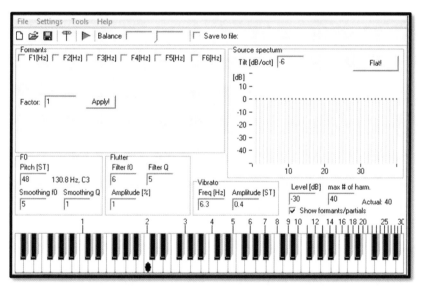

Figure 1: *Madde* voice synthesizer, with vocal tract formants un-checked, showing and playing un-resonated voice source harmonics only.

Madde Exploration 2: the effect of mode of phonation and range on source harmonics.

Deactivate the formant boxes as you did for *Madde* Example 1. To experience the effect of laryngeal register on the voice source, adjust the Tilt [dB/oct] level in the Source spectrum area (upper right) by clicking in the tilt box and using the up and down arrows on your keyboard. The Tilt represents the roll-off in power per octave of the harmonics, the larger the negative number, the greater the tilt. The default Tilt is set for a roll-off of 6 decibels per octave (i.e., -6). A "headier" tone would have a steeper roll off (try -12). A pressed tone would have shallower roll-off (try -3). (This author advises against trying *positive* tilt numbers, at least not with formants deactivated.)

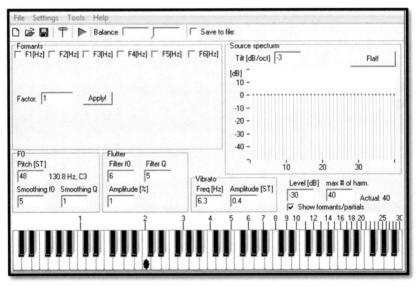

Figure 2: *Madde* voice synthesizer Tilt function (in the Source spectrum box, upper right hand side): Tilt reflects source roll off. Steeper tilt or roll off (a higher negative value) models a headier laryngeal registration. Shallower tilt or roll off (a small negative value) models a chestier laryngeal registration.

Activate the play arrow (top left) for each of these. The steeper the tilt or roll-off, the milder the source will sound, since it will have weaker high harmonics. Since these higher frequencies are precisely where our

118

ears are the most sensitive to intensity, the signal will also sound quieter at steeper tilts (-12), and louder (and more annoying!) at shallower tilts (-3). You will again want to deactivate the sound.

In order to see the effect of pitch on the number of available harmonics, click on successively higher pitches up to soprano high C (C6). The *Madde* keyboard will only show three harmonics at that pitch, since the top C (C8) is missing from its keyboard display. It is dramatically clear that high sopranos face a rather different resonance challenge/ situation than a non-treble male voice faces.

Madde **Exploration 3: formant resonation of source harmonics; harmonic/formant crossings.**

Make sure the "Show formants/partials" box (bottom right just above the keyboard) is checked. Check the formants boxes (upper left, labeled F1[Hz], F2[Hz], F3[Hz], etc.). You will notice a red band appearing for each formant just above its frequency center on the keyboard. You can set the formant frequencies for various voice types and vowels. For example, bass baritone formants for an /e/ vowel

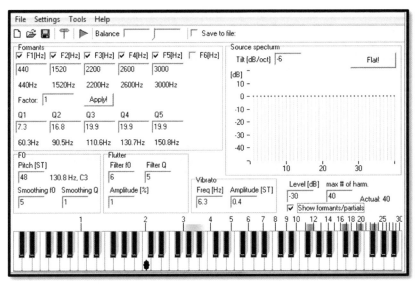

Figure 3: Formants of the vocal tract set for an /e/ in a bass voice.

might be set as follows: F1 440; F2 1520; F3 2200; F4 2600; F5 3000. Set those and play the scale C3 D3 E3 F3 G3. If you continue

119

playing, you may notice timbral changes as harmonics pass through formants (visible just above the keyboard), especially through formant one (more on that later). You will certainly notice that harmonics, once resonated by the vocal tract, are rather more pleasant than with the formants removed. Other vowels can be modeled by varying the frequencies of the first two formants (more on that later).

Madde Exploration 4: open and close timbre.

Make sure the "Show formants/partials" box (bottom right just above the keyboard) is activated. Use the bass baritone formant settings for an /e/ vowel of Exploration 3, Figure 3 above. The first formant for this example is set at A440. Try the following explorations: Play pitches that lie more than an octave below F1 to experience open timbre. Play an ascending scale starting on C3 an octave below middle C. You may notice a timbral "closure" when H3 rises through F1, i.e., from ca. C3 to E3, and even more prominently when H2 rises through

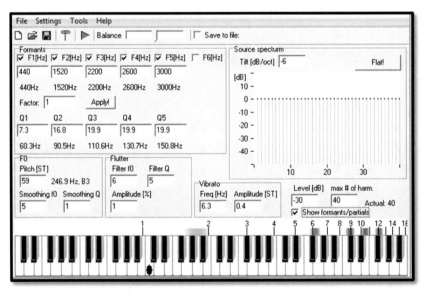

Figure 4. An exploration of turning over, the primary acoustic register transition of a voice, when H2 rises above F1.

F1, from G3 to B3, the primary turning of the voice.

Madde Exploration 5: whoop timbre and beyond.

Make sure the "Show formants/partials" box (bottom right just above the keyboard) is activated. Use the bass baritone formant settings for an /e/ vowel of Example 3, 4 above. The first formant for this example is set at A440. Continue with the following explorations:

1. Ascend stepwise from C4 without adjusting the formants. The implication of leaving the formants the same is that the "singer" is not changing his vocal tract (throat/vowel) shape at all. As H1 approaches F1, the timbre will become increasingly close until full whoop timbre is achieved at the F1/H1 juncture at A4. Notice that this rather falsetto/feminine timbre was achieved with no adjustment to the Source spectrum Tilt, therefore no source change, rather was accomplished entirely by changing harmonic/filter interactions, that is, entirely through changes in resonance. The implication is that source changes (laryngeal registration changes) are not necessarily required for this timbre. It must be noted, however, that in a human subject, source changes are likely to accompany these resonance changes.

2. If you continue to raise H1 above F1 (A4), what is now a countertenor or female "whoop" timbre will quickly thin, demonstrating the necessity of formant tracking above this point.

3. Have the synthesizer "sing" D5. Click on the F1[Hz] box. Repeatedly click the up arrow on your computer keyboard, gradually raising the F1 frequency until it matches D5 (until the red F1 band joins H1 on the pitch D5). You will notice that timbral fullness/depth will return.

4. Click the keyboard down arrow to return F1 to A440 and deactivate the sound.

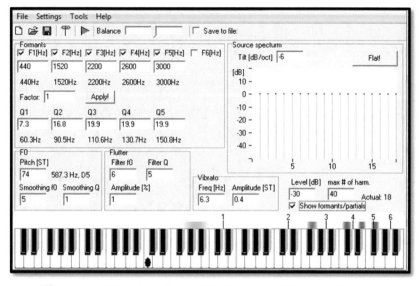

Figure 5. H1 rising above F1 will cause thinness of timbre.

Further *Madde* Explorations

Modeling Exercises and Vocalises

Any of the exercises listed above (see Exploring Vowel Turning, p. 81 and Exploring F1/H1 Tracking, p. 86) can be modeled on *Madde* to demonstrate an approximation of the passive vowel modifications that accompany the primary F1/H2 crossing, or any secondary crossings (F1/H3, F1/H4, etc.) and the timbral fullness of F1/H1 tracking.

F1/F2 Map

Vowels can be more fluidly modeled and changed by selecting "Show F1/F2 map" under the Settings menu. A chart will display with F1 on the horizontal dimension and F2 on the vertical. Clicking and dragging the cursor on this map will manipulate F1 and F2 locations, even while the "voice" is activated. This capability will allow exploration not only of vowels, but also of opening and closing vowels by modifying a vowel to move its first formant across the H2 of the pitch being "sung."

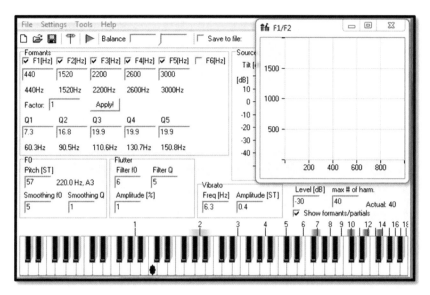

Figure 6. F1/F2 map (Vowel Formant Map)

Modeling Student Voices

If a student's formants (from a comfortable part of the range) are derived, perhaps by using *VoceVista*, the student's voice can be modeled in *Madde* for further exploration. For example, the passive vowel modifications of a young male singer's primary register transition on various vowels can be modeled. While it is not usually necessary to model a specific voice to begin to understand passive modification, it may be helpful for some. More often a generic model of the same voice type will suffice. Also F1/H1 tracking of treble voices can be convincingly demonstrated, and the resultant active vowel modifications.

Appendix 2: Approximate F1 Locations by Voice

Why *Approximate* First Formant Locations?

The chart on the following page gives *approximate* first formant locations by general voice type. The formant boxes are deliberately non-specific (covering more than one pitch) for several reasons: general voice types have varieties of subdivisions that accommodate some variety of vocal tract length, which overlap with adjacent voice types and subdivisions. For example, a high lyric baritone may have formants that are higher than those of a *Heldentenor*, or a deeper mezzosoprano may have formants that are lower than those of a *leggiero* tenor. Voices are individual, as are their formant locations. However first formant locations will not vary very far from the approximate locations given, and the general contour of formant locations from vowel to vowel will be relatively stable. One could use *VoceVista* to identify specific spoken formants or formants of vowels sung near speech range if specificity is desired. However, the teacher's ear and the ease and efficiency of vocal function are usually sufficient for refining the locations of acoustic registration events. Once a teacher knows approximate locations by voice type, the passive vowel modifications that accompany these events, and strategies to encourage timbral consistency (i.e., tube length stability) across these events, the student's vocal function will guide further adjustments.

Approximate F1 Locations by Voice

See www.kenbozeman.com

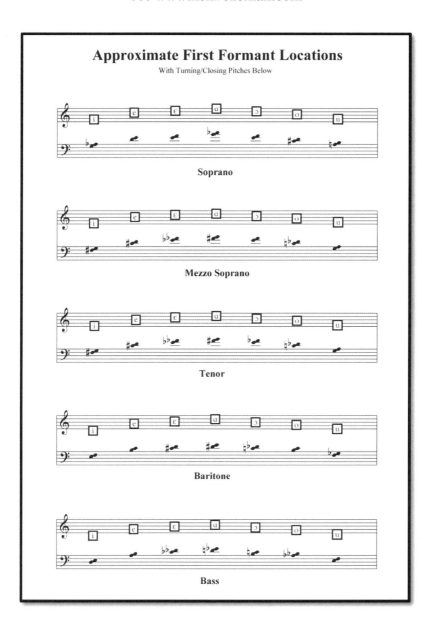

Appendix 3: Events Surrounding the Male *Passaggio*

See www.kenbozeman.com

126

Appendix 4: DVD Contents

(Now available at: http://www.kenbozeman.com)

These sample explorations were made in the year of publication with available undergraduate students at various levels of development. While they model the acoustic phenomena being discussed reasonably well, neither they nor the author would claim that they represent singers whose training is completed. The author is very grateful for their willingness to serve as models for educational purposes.

Exploring Vowel Turning (see chapter 13, p. 81)

Example 1. Leaps across the turn

Example 2. Leaping and stepping across the turn

Example 3. Levels of turning

Example 4. Repeated note from close to open to close

Example 5. Same vowel across multiple levels

Example 6. Turning with agility

Example 7. Descending and ascending through the turn

Example 8. Ascending and descending through the turn

Exploring F1/H1 Tracking (see chapter 13, p. 86)

Example 9.   Repeated note

Example 10. Leap up to open vowel, repeated to close vowel

Example 11. Leap up on same vowel

Example 12. Stepwise Ascent and Descent

Appendix 5: Youtube Examples:

(Now available at: http://www.kenbozeman.com)

There is inherent risk in citing Youtube examples, including the potential instability of the cited locations. At the time of this printing, these cited locations had been stably available for a number of years. Their educational value overruled the author's concerns about their potential instability. Most of the recordings cited can also be found in other formats. (Youtube titles in **bold**.)

Example 1: **Leontyne Price "Beim Schlafengehen " Strauss' Vier Letzte Lieder**

http://www.youtube.com/watch?v=w1FePUXk_io&t=0m39s

Example 2: **Nicolai Gedda canta Rachmaninov II**

http://www.youtube.com/watch?v=AFa9hgb0tmI&t=2m50s

Example 3: **José Van Dam sings Kaddish by Ravel**

http://www.youtube.com/watch?v=IAiWPrhxlpc&t=3m45s

Example 4: **Jussi Björling, Ah, Love But A Day**

Piano version: http://www.youtube.com/watch?v=li6aAo47uew

Orchestral version: **Jussi Björling sings "Ah Love, but a day"**

http://www.youtube.com/watch?v=4TWoHdA085g&t=0m23s

Example 5: **Jussi Bjorling - "Ombra mai fu"- Atlanta 1959**

http://www.youtube.com/watch?feature=endscreen&NR=1&v=KAI4mS-SUYM&t=1m52s

128

Example 6: **George London sings Schubert -- "An die Musik"**

http://www.youtube.com/watch?v=rusv0pP_qqw&list=PL97752B1A98F35CB1&t=0m7s

Example 7: **Pavarotti about covered sound**

http://www.youtube.com/watch?v=uo6dDQiBGyI&feature=endscreen&NR=1

Example 8: **How to sing bel canto 2/2** (see 0:30-1:15):

http://www.youtube.com/watch?v=XPplK22nSXY&t=0m30s

Example 9: **How to sing bel canto 1/2** (see 3:14-3:55):

http://www.youtube.com/watch?v=3nH54BdqWpg&t=3m14s

Example 10: **Rockwell Blake describes dark timbre and passaggio.flv**

http://www.youtube.com/watch?v=0XcWCUNaX04

Selected References

Austin, Stephen F. "The *voce chiusa*." *Journal of Singing*. March/April 2005; Vol. 61, No. 4: 421-425.

Bourne, T., Garnier, M., Kenny, D. "Music Theater Voice: Production, Physiology and Pedagogy." *Journal of Singing*. March/April 2011; Vol 67, No. 4: 237-244.

Bozeman, Kenneth. "A Case for Voice Science in the Voice Studio." *Journal of Singing*. Jan/Feb 2007; Vol. 63, No. 3:265–270.

Bozeman, Kenneth. "Acoustic *passaggio* pedagogy for the male voice." *Logopedics Phoniatrics Vocology*. 2012 Early Online. 1-6.

Bozeman, Kenneth. "New Technology for Teaching Voice Science and Pedagogy: The Madde Synthesizer (Svante Granqvist)." *Journal of Singing*. Mar/Apr 2012; Vol. 68, No. 4:415–418.

Bozeman, Kenneth. "On the Voice: Registration Strategies for Training the Male *Passaggio*." *Choral Journal*. June/July, 2008; 48:59-72.

Bozeman, Kenneth. "The Role of the First Formant in Training the Male Singing Voice." *Journal of Singing*. Jan/Feb 2010; Vol. 66, No. 3:291-297.

Delvaux, Bertrand, Howard, David. "A New Method to Explore the Spectral Impact of the Piriform Fossae on the Singing Voice: Benchmarking Using MRI-Based 3D-Printed Vocal Tracts." PLoS ONE 9(7): e102680.doi:10.1371/journal.pone.0102680. July 21, 2014.

Herbst, Christian T., Švec, Jan G. "Adjustment of glottal configurations in singing." *Journal of Singing* (Jan/Feb 2014).

Herbst, Christian T., Howard, David, Švec, Jan G. "The sound source in singing—basic principles and muscular adjustments for fine-tuning vocal timbre." in: *The Oxford Handbook of Singing*. Oxford University Press, D. Howard, J. Nix, G. Welch Eds.

Ladefoged, Peter. *Elements of acoustic phonetics*, Chicago, Il: University of Chicago Press; 1962.

Lovetri, Jeanette. "The Confusion about Belting: a Personal Observation." *VoicePrints: Journal of the New York Singing Teachers' Association* September-October 2012, pp. 4-7.

McCoy, Scott. *Your Voice, An Inside View,* Princeton, NJ: Inside View Press; 2012.

McKinney, James. *The Diagnosis and Correction of Vocal Faults.* San Diego, CA: Singular Press: 1982.

Miller, Donald G. *Registers of the Singing Voice,* Groningen, Netherlands: Groningen Press; 2000.

Miller, Donald G. *Resonance in Singing,* Princeton, NJ: Inside View Press; 2008.

Miller, Richard. *The Structure of Singing: System and Art in Vocal Technique.* New York: Schirmer Books; 1986.

Nair, Garyth. *The Craft of Singing,* San Diego, CA: Plural Publishing; 2007.

Nair, Garyth. *Voice—Tradition and Technology,* San Diego, CA: Singular Publishing Group; 1999.

Schutte, Harm K., Miller, Donald, G. "Belting and Pop, Nonclassical Approaches to Female Middle Voice: Some Preliminary Considerations." *Journal of Voice.* 7(2) (1993): 142-150.

Schutte, Harm K., Miller, Donald, G. "Mixing Registers: Glottal Source or Vocal Tract." *Folia Phoniatrica et Logopaedica.* 57 (2005): 278-291.

Schutte, Harm K., Miller, Donald, G. "Physical Definition of the Flageolet Register." *Journal of Voice.* 7(3) (1993): 206-212.

Schutte, Harm K., Miller, Donald, G. "Resonance Strategies Revealed in Recorded Tenor High Notes." *Folia Phoniatrica et Logopaedica.* 57 (2005): 292-307.

Schutte, Harm K., Miller, Donald, G., Švec, Jan G. "Measurement of Formant Frequencies and Bandwidths in Singing." *Journal of Voice.* 9(3) (1995): 290-296.

Steinhauer, Kimberly M., and Estill, Jo. "The Estill Voice Model: Physiology of Emotion," *Voice and Emotion*, Vol. 2, Chapter 6, Plural Publishing; 2008. pp 83-99.

Sundberg, Johan. "Articulatory interpretation of the singing formants," *Journal of the Acoustical Society of America,* 55 (1974): 838 – 844.

Sundberg, Johan. "Level and Center Frequency of the Singer's Formant," *Journal of Voice*, 15(2) (2001): 176-186.

Sundberg, Johan. *The Science of the Singing Voice*, Imprint DeKalb, Ill.: Northern Illinois University Press, 1987.

Titze, Ingo. *Principles of Voice Production*, Englewood Cliffs, N.J.: Prentice Hall, 1994.

Titze, Ingo., & Story, Brad. "Acoustic interactions of the voice source with the lower vocal tract," *Journal of the Acoustical Society of America*, 101(4) (1997): 2234-2243.

Titze, Ingo & Verdolini Abbott, Katherine. *Vocology: The Science and Practice of Voice Habilitation*, Salt Lake City, Utah: The National Center for Voice & Speech, 2012.

Index

front, 9, 16, 107

modification, 13, 25, 27, 28, 30, 33, 34, 40-43, 49-51, 74-76, 97, 112, 115, 122, 123

open, 14, 22, 26, 33, 106, 111

placement sensations, 66, 67

turning, 39, 40, 45-48, 51-53, 59, 60, 81-89

yell, 21-25, 37, 68-71, 80, 104, 107, 115

coupling, 115

instinct, 39, 45, 76, 90, 92

timbre, 28, 71, 114, 115